300
PAPER-PIECED
Quilt Blocks

300
PAPER-PIECED
Quilt Blocks
CAROL DOAK

Martingale®
& C O M P A N Y

CREDITS

President	NANCY J. MARTIN
CEO	DANIEL J. MARTIN
Publisher	JANE HAMADA
Editorial Director	MARY V. GREEN
Managing Editor	TINA COOK
Technical Editor	URSULA REIKES
Copy Editor	ELLEN BALSTAD
Design Director	STAN GREEN
Illustrator	LAUREL STRAND
Cover and Text Designer	TRINA STAHL
Photographer	BRENT KANE

That Patchwork Place® is an imprint of Martingale & Company®.

300 Paper-Pieced Quilt Blocks
© 2004 by Carol Doak

Martingale & Company
20205 144th Avenue NE
Woodinville, WA 98072-8478 USA
www.martingale-pub.com

Printed in China
09 08 07 06 05 04   8 7 6 5 4 3 2 1

MISSION STATEMENT

Dedicated to providing quality products and service to inspire creativity.

Library of Congress Cataloging-in-Publication Data

Doak, Carol.
    300 paper-pieced quilt blocks / Carol Doak.
        p. cm.
    ISBN 1-56477-534-8
    1. Patchwork—Patterns. 2. Quilting. I. Title: Three hundred paper-pieced quilt blocks. II. Title.
    TT835.D59143 2004
    746.46'041—dc22

2004010490

DEDICATION

This book is dedicated to all of those quilters who love to paper piece!

ACKNOWLEDGMENTS

I extend my heartfelt thank-yous and appreciation to the following people:

Sherry Reis for being a supportive friend and for not telling me that a 300-block book was a huge endeavor;

Ursula Reikes for her dear friendship and for her wonderful expertise during the production of this book;

Bernina Sewing Machines for a sewing machine that I could always count on when I sewed all of these blocks;

Timeless Treasures Fabrics for beautiful fabrics that I used in some of the sample blocks; and

Everyone at Martingale & Company for their support, friendship, and all that they did to create this beautiful book.

CONTENTS

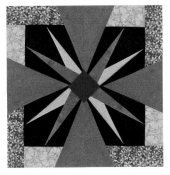   

INTRODUCTION

Paper piecing is a wonderful method to produce accurate patchwork even if you are a beginner. The paper supports the fabric so that it will not stretch, and you do not have to cut the fabric pieces to the exact size or sew with a perfect ¼" seam allowance. Simply sew on the lines following the numbered sequence and you can be assured of wonderful results!

I have been designing paper-pieced projects for more than a decade now, and I have wanted a single resource for a large group of block designs. That longing was the inspiration for this big book of paper-pieced block designs. Except for the alphabet, these block designs have not been published in my previous books, so they will offer new inspirations for your patchwork projects.

The beginning portion of this book covers paper-piecing supplies and describes how to make your paper foundations. I am so pleased that we are able to include with this book a CD-ROM that will let you print your foundations from your personal computer. Even if you are not a computer person, this easy-to-use program will have you printing your foundations in minutes.

Fabric cutting and cutting lists are covered next. Although each block design includes a cutting list specifying the correct size to cut fabric pieces, information about determining fabric-piece sizes is covered in the event you decide to print your foundations in a different size. I also include information regarding calculating yardage for your paper-pieced project and some speed-cutting techniques. I am always eager to get started on my projects, so cutting the fabric pieces easily and quickly is important to me.

The step-by-step paper-piecing instructions (page 12) will take you from piece #1 to the trimming of your block. They feature easy directions and include photographs just in case you are a "show me" person. Don't overlook the paper-piecing techniques and tips because they will assist you in your paper-piecing endeavors. I suggest that you read through the beginning portion of this book a couple of times before making your first paper-pieced block because it will help establish the process for you.

The majority of the blocks are presented in a 4" format and begin on page 43. The alphabet and number blocks are presented in a 3" format because that size is appropriate for creating words within a quilt. The gallery pages following the alphabet and number blocks (pages 29–42) show the 4" blocks in four-block groups. Use the gallery pages to find the number of the block you want to make and its page number. This will not only give you an easy way to peruse the hundreds of blocks, but it will also provide inspiration for putting the same blocks in a quilt. You will have opportunities to put blocks together to create different images. Take the time to play with your options because the results can be so varied.

I've included a wide variety of block designs, from everyday items like houses, trees, and fences, to seacoast themes, holidays, hearts, florals, and geometric-style blocks. The number of pieces per block varies greatly from block to block. Some blocks have as few as five pieces and will work up very quickly. Don't shy away from a block with more pieces. It is not more difficult; it will only take longer to make.

I often see wonderful projects made from patterns in my previous books. It is such a pleasure for me to see how quilters can take a design and make it their own with fabric choices and placement. I am looking forward to seeing the creative projects produced from this large resource of paper-pieced block designs.

Until next time, all the best,

Carol

Using the right tools and supplies to paper piece makes the process of paper piecing easy and fun. The following items will do just that.

6" Add-A-Quarter ruler: This tool is invaluable for pretrimming the fabric pieces so that you will know exactly where to place the next pieces of fabric (see "Resources" on page 175).

6" Add-An-Eighth ruler: This tool is used in the same manner as the Add-A-Quarter ruler but with paper piecing miniature blocks or pieces (see "Resources").

Foundation paper: Use a lightweight newsprint paper when you print or copy the paper-piecing designs.

Olfa rotary point cutter: Use this tool to undo seams easily (see page 15).

Open-toe presser foot: This foot provides good visibility so that you can see the line as you sew.

Postcard: Use a sturdy postcard or 3" x 5" card to fold the paper back on the next sewing line before trimming the previously sewn fabric piece(s).

Rotary cutter and rotary mat: Choose a large rotary cutter that will allow you to cut through several layers of fabric.

Rotary rulers: The 6" x 12" and the 6" x 6" rotary rulers are helpful for cutting the fabric and trimming the blocks.

Sandpaper tabs: Place stick-on sandpaper tabs (available at your local quilt shop) every 3" along the length and ½" from the edge of the rotary ruler. This will prevent the ruler from slipping on the paper when you trim.

Scotch-brand removable tape: This tape will be helpful if you need to repair a foundation or resew across a previously sewn line.

Sewing thread: Use a standard 50-weight sewing thread. Match the thread to the general color value of the fabrics. In most cases, you can rely upon white, medium gray, and black thread.

Silk pins with small heads or flat-headed pins: Because you will be pinning your first piece and then placing the postcard on top of the pin, use pins with small or flat heads that won't get in your way.

Size 90/14 sewing-machine needles: This larger needle will help to perforate the paper foundation, making it easy to remove later.

Small stick-on notes: Label your fabric pieces with these notes to keep organized.

Stapler and staple remover: Use a stapler to secure several foundations for trimming, and a staple remover to remove the staple after the foundations are trimmed.

Thread clippers: A pair of thread clippers with narrow, curved blades will assist you in clipping threads from the top and bottom of the foundation at the same time (see page 15). See "Resources" on page 175 to obtain more information about this tool.

Tweezers: Use tweezers to remove small bits of paper caught in the intersecting seams.

PAPER FOUNDATIONS

Each foundation-pieced block requires a paper foundation. One way to make these paper foundations is to photocopy the designs on a copy machine. Be sure to check the accuracy of the machine against the original, and make all your copies for each project on the same copy machine from the original design. For a nominal fee, most copy shops will remove the binding of this book and three-hole punch the pages or spiral bind it to make using it on a copy machine even easier.

A copy machine that has the capability to reduce or enlarge offers the opportunity to create the blocks in a variety of sizes. The following chart shows the result of reduction and enlargement percentages.

3" BLOCK SIZE

Percentage of Enlargement or Reduction	New Block Size
50%	1½"
66%	2"
83%	2½"
116%	3½"
133%	4"

4" BLOCK SIZE

Percentage of Enlargement or Reduction	New Block Size
75%	3"
87%	3½"
112%	4½"
125%	5"
137%	5½"
150%	6"

Another easy way to make the foundation copies is to use your computer to print them. I am thrilled, delighted, and ecstatic that I am able to include a CD-ROM with this book that will allow you to use your home computer to print the block designs. I know that for some of you, the word *computer* is a four-letter word, but trust me—you will love having the ability to print these designs in the size you like and to have multiples of the same design (depending upon its size) on a page. The installation process for this program is simple. Once installed, you just point and click on the design you would like to print. This will bring you to the print page, where you indicate your choices prior to printing. There is a help section in the program that describes all your options with pictures and customer support from Quilt-Pro Systems should you need it. Information about the system requirements and installation of this computer program is on the inside of the back cover.

The foundation paper you use should hold up during the sewing process and be easy to remove when the project is complete. If in doubt, test your paper by sewing through it with a size 90/14 needle and a stitch length of 18 to 20 stitches per inch. On a sewing machine with a range of 0-5, this would be a 1½. If the paper tears as you sew, it is not strong enough. If it doesn't tear easily when pulled after sewing, it is too strong. The paper does not need to be translucent. You can use it as long as the light from your sewing machine allows you to see through the blank side of the paper to the lines on the other side.

After you make the necessary copies, cut the blocks ½" from the outside sewing line. To do this quickly and easily when printing several of the same block designs on more than one page, staple the center of each foundation through all like pages. Use your rotary cutter to trim the stapled foundations ½" from the solid outside line. Remove the staple.

FABRIC

ecause you are sewing to a paper foundation, your fabric pieces do not need to be on the straight grain because they are supported by the foundation. However, fabric grain is important for visual reasons. In some cases, the same fabric will be placed along seam lines going in different directions, causing the grain of the fabric to go in different directions. Choose nondirectional print fabrics for background areas to avoid seeing the print go in several different directions. In the following block example, nondirectional white fabric was used in the background area. For the design elements inside the block, you may choose directional prints because they will be consistent with the other blocks and will not be distracting. In the block example, I chose a black-and-white check fabric for the center strip. This fabric works fine as a design element, and when four blocks are placed together, it is consistent.

Block 161 with nondirectional background

Four blocks set together

CUTTING LISTS

he good news about paper piecing is that you do not need to cut your fabric pieces to the exact size. They just need to be large enough to fill the area on the pattern plus a generous seam allowance after the fabric is sewn and flipped. A cutting list, with its fabric-piece sizes and piece location information, is an efficient resource when cutting your fabric pieces and labeling them by location before you begin to sew. In this book, I created the cutting lists and made the blocks from the sizes listed.

Measuring Fabric-Piece Size

If you change your block size from the one listed in this book, enlarging or reducing it, you will need to create a new cutting list to fit your new block size. Therefore, you will want to know how to measure for the correct-size fabric pieces.

To measure for piece #1, place your ruler over piece #1 in the same way you intend to place your fabric. Look through the ruler to determine how large the piece needs to be, and then add a generous seam allowance. I rely upon the approximate size plus ¾" total for seam allowances. In the following example, piece #1 would be cut 2¾" x 4¾".

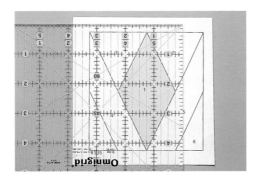

To measure subsequent pieces, place the ¼" line of the ruler on the line you will sew and let the ruler fall over the piece you are measuring. Look through the ruler to determine the needed size plus a generous seam allowance on all sides. For example, to measure for piece #2 shown in the photo below, place the ¼" ruler line on the seam line between piece #1 and piece #2 in the same way you will place the fabric. Looking through the ruler, you will see that you should cut a piece 2½" x 3".

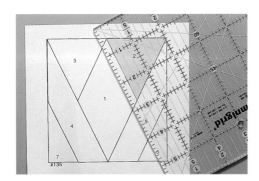

To measure for half-square triangles (straight grain on the short side of the triangle), measure the short side of the triangle and cut a square 1¼" larger.

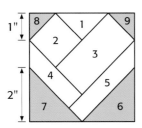

Cut this square once diagonally to make two half-square triangles.

To measure the square size for pieces #6 and #7, add 2" plus 1¼" for a 3¼" square. Cut this square once diagonally for two half-square triangles.

To measure the square size for pieces #8 and #9, add 1" plus 1¼" for a 2¼" square. Cut this square once diagonally for two half-square triangles.

To measure quarter-square triangles (straight grain on the long side of the triangle), measure the long side of the triangle and cut a square 1½" larger.

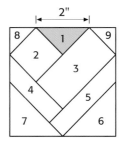

Cut this square twice diagonally to make four quarter-square triangles.

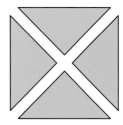

To measure the square size for piece #1, add 2" plus 1½" for a 3½" square. Cut this square twice diagonally for four quarter-square triangles.

CREATING A NEW CUTTING LIST

As you take your measurements, write them down on your block foundation. List the size to cut and the location(s) where this size will be used. List the biggest cut sizes first so that the smaller pieces can be cut from the remaining larger portions of a strip.

CALCULATING FABRIC YARDAGE

Since you will be using these blocks in projects, I want to share with you these easy steps to calculate yardage for a project.

1. Determine the number of blocks you will make.

2. Multiply the number of the first cut size for a particular fabric times the number of blocks you will make to determine the total number of this cut size for your project. For example, if one block requires 2 rectangles, each 2" x 4", and you are making 40 blocks for your project, you would cut 80 pieces, each 2" x 4".

3. Divide the width of fabric (I use 42") by the length of each cut piece. In our example, divide 42" (width of the fabric) by 4" (the length of our piece) to determine that we can cut 10 pieces from each strip of fabric. Use only the whole number of your answer, since you cannot cut part of a needed size.

4. Determine the number of strips to cut by dividing the number you can cut from one strip (our answer was 10) into the number of pieces you need to cut. For example, divide 80 (the number needed) by 10 (the number that can be cut from one strip), which equals 8 strips to cut.

5. Multiply the number of strips to cut (8 in our example) by the width of each strip you will cut (2" in our example) to determine that you will need 16" of fabric. Increase this amount up to 18" or ½ yard to provide a bit of extra fabric just in case.

If you are cutting more than one size from the fabric, calculate the additional sizes in the same way. Add the yardages to determine the total yardage needed for the fabric. The following chart will assist you in determining the number of each length that can be cut from a 42"-wide strip.

PIECE YIELDS FROM A 42"-WIDE STRIP

Cut Lengths	Number of Pieces
1"	42
1¼"	33
1½"	28
1¾"	24
2"	21
2¼"	18
2½"	16
2¾"	15
3"	14
3¼"	12
3½"	12
3¾"	11
4"	10
4¼"	9
4½"	9
4¾"	8
5"	8
5¼"	8
5½"	7
6"	7
6¼"	6
6½"	6
7"	6
7¼"	5

Speed Cutting

Once you cut your strips, you can layer them to cut multiple layers at one time. You can layer up to four folded strips (or eight layers) in each stack. When more than four strips are involved, align the subsequent layered strips along the long edge of the first group of strips. In the previous example, we cut eight 2"-wide strips. The following illustrations show how two sets of four strips would be layered to cut the 4" lengths.

As you cut each size from each fabric, label the stacks with the location numbers given in the cutting

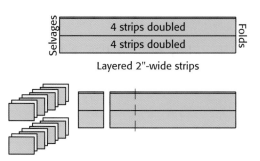

Layered 2"-wide strips

list. Do take the time to stack all of the fabric pieces right side up because it will speed up the piecing process.

Paper-Piecing Techniques

Once you've made a paper foundation, cut your fabric pieces, and labeled them with the location number for the block, you are ready to paper piece.

Step-by-Step Paper Piecing

I will describe the paper-piecing process by using just one block, but you can sew the same blocks in an assembly-line approach without cutting the thread between the blocks. So that you can see through the blocks in the following photos, I have used transparent paper for the foundations.

1. Use a 90/14 sewing-machine needle, an open-toe presser foot for good visibility, and a stitch length of 18 to 20 stitches per inch. This is approximately 1.5 on a sewing machine that has a stitch-length range of 0-5. The larger needle and smaller stitch length will allow you to remove the paper easily.

2. Using the light on your sewing machine, look through the blank side of the paper to place piece #1 right side up over the area marked #1. Turn the paper over and make sure it covers area #l and extends at least ¼" beyond all seam lines. Pin in place using small-headed or flat-headed pins.

Place the pin parallel to the seam line between areas #1 and #2.

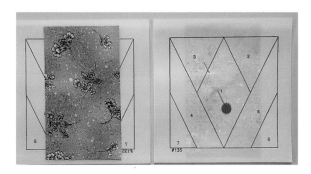

3. Place the postcard on the line between areas #1 and #2, and fold the paper back to expose the excess fabric beyond the seam line.

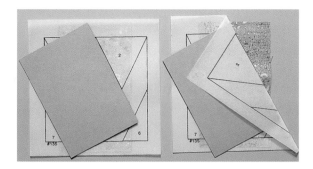

4. Place the Add-A-Quarter ruler on the fold and trim the excess fabric ¼" from the fold. The lip on the ruler prevents it from slipping as you trim.

Or you can align the ¼" line on a rotary ruler with the fold to trim ¼" from the fold.

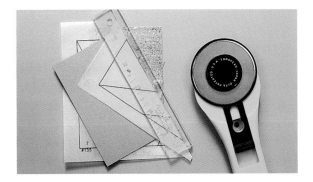

5. Looking through the blank side of the paper to the design on the other side, place piece #2 right side up over area #2. This is an important step. The reason you want to look through the blank side of the paper to position the next piece of fabric is to see how the fabric will appear after it is sewn and pressed open. Remember, what you see is what you get.

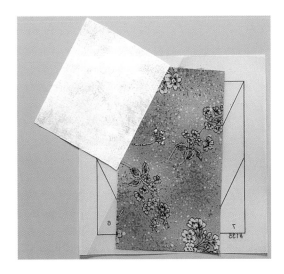

After piece #2 is properly positioned, flip it right sides together with the just-trimmed edge of piece #1. Looking through the blank side of the paper again, check that the ends of piece #2 extend beyond the seam lines of area #2 on the foundation. In the following example, I have placed red arrows to indicate the end of the seam line for piece #2. See how the fabric has been placed to extend beyond the widest part of piece #2 to provide a seam allowance?

If you are using cotton fabric, piece #2 should cling to piece #1, but if it makes you more comfortable, you can pin piece #2 in place. If

you are using slippery fabrics such as satins, definitely pin piece #2 in place.

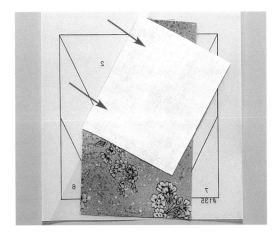

6. Place the foundation under the presser foot and sew on the seam line between areas #1 and #2, beginning about ½" before the seam and extending the stitching about the same distance beyond the end of the seam.

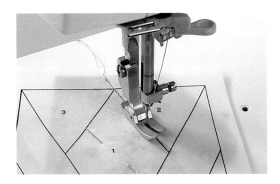

7. Clip the threads (see tip on page 15). Remove the pin and open piece #2. If you are using cotton fabrics, press with a dry iron on the cotton setting. If you are using heat-sensitive fabrics, use a pressing cloth or lower the temperature on the iron. Cover your ironing surface with a piece of scrap fabric to protect it from any ink that may transfer from the photocopies or printer copies.

8. Place the postcard on the next line you will sew. This is where piece #3 adjoins the previous piece(s). Fold the paper back, exposing the excess fabrics. With this seam, it will be necessary to pull the stitches away from the foundation to fold the paper and that is okay. Place the Add-A-Quarter ruler on the fold and trim ¼" from the fold.

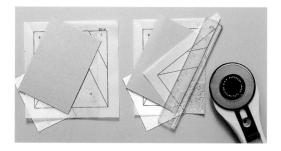

9. Place piece #3 right side up over area #3 to check for proper placement. Place the fabric right sides together with the just-trimmed edge of piece #1. See how the fabric extends on both ends for adequate seam allowances? Sew, clip threads, and press open.

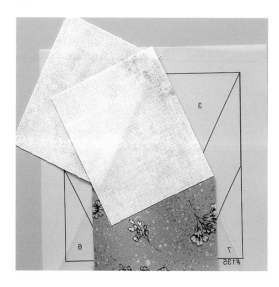

10. Continue with piece #4 by placing the postcard on the line where piece #4 joins pieces #1 and #3. Fold the paper back and trim the excess fabric ¼" from the fold. Place piece #4 right side up over area #4 to check for proper placement; then flip it right sides together along the just-trimmed edge. Sew and press open.

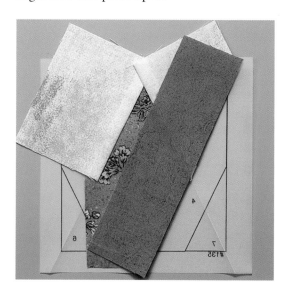

11. Continue in the same manner until all of the pieces have been added. Using the rotary ruler, align the ¼" line on the outside sewing line and trim the paper foundation and fabrics ¼" from the sewing line on all sides.

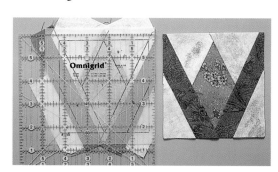

Do not remove the paper yet. Remove the paper after you join the blocks to other blocks or fabric so that the edges will be stabilized. To remove the paper, gently tug against the stitching line, and the fabric will pull away from the stitching. To remove the paper strips in the seam allowance, use a pair of tweezers. Do not fret about removing every tiny bit of paper; it will only add to the warmth of your quilt.

Paper-Piecing Tips

The following tips will assist you in making paper piecing a breeze.

- When placing a right triangle on the foundation, place it right side up first and then flip it right sides together with the just-trimmed edge. To center the triangle, align the right-angle corner on the foundation with the right-angle corner on the fabric.

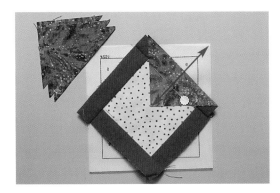

Aligning triangles

- A super way to add a bit of detail to your paper-pieced block is to center a fabric element over area #1 of the block. In the following example, the flowerpot was centered to represent a label on the jar. To center a design element, place the fabric over area #1 in your desired location by looking through a light source and pin in place. Paper piece in the usual fashion.

Using fabric motifs

- Set up a pressing area next to your sewing machine. You can even lower an ironing board to make a convenient area to press. Cover your ironing surface with a piece of scrap fabric since some of the ink from the copies may transfer when pressing.

- Use a small travel iron (preferably without steam holes) set on the cotton setting. If you are using heat-sensitive fabrics, adjust the iron temperature accordingly, or use a pressing cloth.

- Sew blocks that are the same in an assembly-line approach without cutting the threads in between. This will speed up the paper-piecing process.

- With the paper side facing up, pull up on the top thread and it will pull the bobbin thread up slightly. Using curved, pointed snips, clip close to the surface of the foundation to cut the top and bobbin thread at the same time. This neat method will save you time clipping threads.

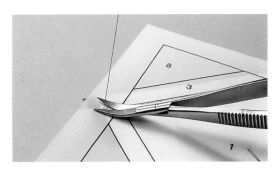

Clipping thread with curved snips

- If it is necessary to repair a torn foundation or restitch a line, use Scotch-brand removable tape. If you should run out of bobbin thread while sewing and need to restitch the same line, use the tape along the seam line so that the foundation will not tear when sewn again. Do not touch your iron directly to the tape.

- If it is necessary to remove a line of stitching, place a piece of Scotch-brand removable tape on the stitching line you need to remove. Pull the top fabric piece back to expose the thread. Lightly touch the point of an Olfa rotary point cutter to the threads, keeping tension on the fabric as the threads are cut. This method of removing stitches not only goes quickly, but the tape provides a good foundation for resewing the seam line.

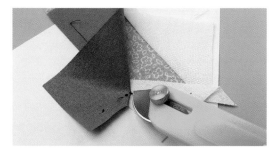

Removing stitches

ADDING PIECED UNITS

Some paper-pieced designs have pieced units. When a pieced unit is indicated, one number is assigned to the unit followed by letters, such as 2a and 2b. Two slashes (//) are placed on the seam(s) that need to be pieced before adding the unit to the foundation. The pieced units are made up of fabric pieces that you sew together before adding them to the foundation. Pieced units may have one or more seams.

When there is only one seam in a pieced unit, sew the two pieces of fabric together prior to joining them as one unit to the foundation. In the following example, the window and house fabrics for piece #4a (house) and piece #4b (window) are joined as a pieced unit before they are joined as one unit to the foundation. Position the horizontal seam on the line seen through the blank side of the paper and pin the unit in place. Machine baste on the seam line between piece #3 and pieced unit #4 for about ½", crossing over the horizontal seam. Check for a good match, and then sew the seam. Press the unit open and baste it to the foundation along the vertical seam line for about 1", crossing over the horizontal seam line so that it will not move when you join the next fabric piece to the foundation.

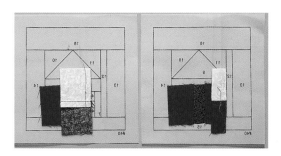

Making and adding a pieced unit
that has a single seam

When there is more than one seam in a pieced unit, the easiest and most accurate way to make the unit is right on the foundation prior to paper piecing the block. As a reminder to make these multiseam pieced units on the foundation, I have placed an asterisk symbol following the number and the letter *a* for these units. In the following example, piece #6a* is placed on the foundation as if it were piece #1, and piece #6b and piece #6c are joined to piece #6a*. Fold the paper back on the line where pieced unit #6 will join piece #5, and trim the pieced unit ¼" from the line. Place Scotch-brand removable tape on the stitched seam lines and gently remove the pieced unit.

Paper piece the block and, when it is time to join pieced unit #6 to the foundation, position it in place by matching the seams with the lines on the foundation. Pin pieced unit #6 in place and machine baste across the matching seams. Check for a good match and sew. Press the unit open and machine baste the free edge to the foundation for about 1" so that the joined seams will not move.

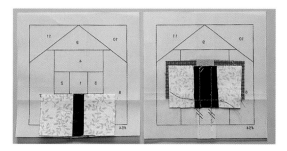

Making and adding a pieced unit that has a multiple seam

Joining Blocks or Block Sections

To join completed and trimmed blocks accurately, place the blocks right sides together and use your tabletop to align the edge you will join. Pin at the beginning of the block and at any matching points. Also pin every 3" along the edge if there are no matching points and at the end of the block.

If you are joining irregularly shaped sections, place a pin through the beginning of the line in one section through to the beginning of the line in the other section underneath. Repeat the same procedure for the end of the line. This will align the sewing line so that it can be pinned accurately.

To see if the lines will match up when sewn, place the sewing-machine needle through the line approximately in the middle of the block and punch a hole through to the bottom block. If the hole is not also on the line, adjust your pinning before proceeding.

To ensure a good match and to prevent the foundations from shifting when sewing, machine baste at the beginning and at any matching points. Also baste every 3" along the seam line if there are no matching points and at the end. Check that you have a good match. If you would like to adjust any point along the seam, simply clip the basting thread on the top and bottom on each side of that point, and remove it from the bobbin side. Adjust and rebaste for a good match.

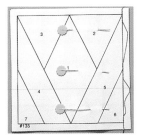

Once you are satisfied with your seam, sew the seam on the line with a small stitch. When joining block sections, press intersecting seam allowances in opposing directions.

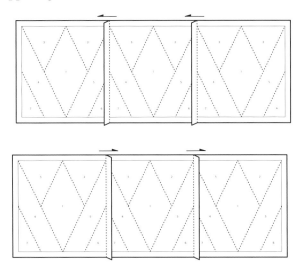

A few of the block designs in this book require that you paper piece each section partially, join the sections, and complete the paper piecing across the joined sections. This method is indicated when the same number is used in both sections and dotted lines appear at the seam lines, as shown in the following illustration. Prior to joining the sections, trim ¼" from the seam lines at the points where you will add the final pieces. In the illustration, the red arrows indicate the seam lines that should be trimmed to ¼" before joining the two sections. Note that if you do not trim before joining the sections, you will not be able to do it after the sections are joined because the seam allowance will be caught in the joining seam.

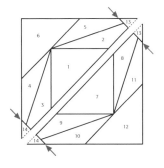 

Block 235
Join the two halves and then add pieces #13 and #14 across the joined foundations.

EMBELLISHMENTS

Embellishments such as the appliquéd wheels on the vehicle blocks can be made by using a circle template to cut the wheel shapes from fabric. I used a fusible web to attach these shapes to the block. You can also cut circles, adding seam allowances, and hand appliqué them to your block. Buttons would be another alternative for wheels.

Facial details for the little girl blocks and bunny block were simply drawn on the fabric with a permanent pen. If you prefer, you can embroider these details.

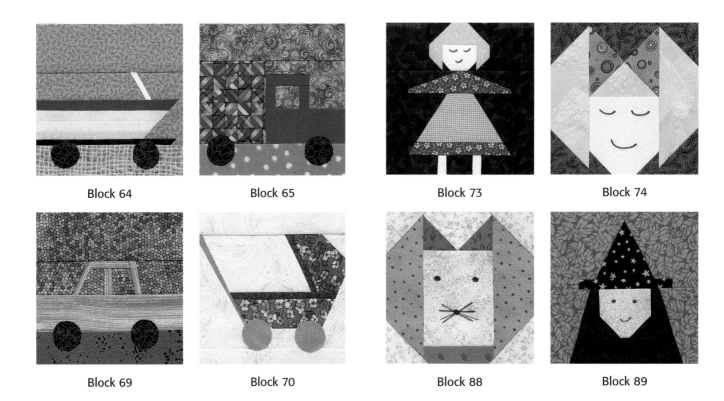

Block 64   Block 65   Block 73   Block 74

Block 69   Block 70   Block 88   Block 89

For wheels, appliqué fabric circles to the pieced blocks or stitch on buttons for a dimensional look.

Draw facial features with a permanent marker or embroider them with floss.

ABOUT THE BLOCKS

The alphabet blocks and number blocks are presented in a 3" size because this is a workable size for including words in your quilt.

The 4" blocks, which cover a variety of themes, are shown on pages 43–174 beside their foundation patterns. The gallery on pages 29–42 demonstrates how the designs could work in a quilt project, with four of each block set in a grouping. I encourage you to be creative with positioning options.

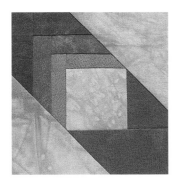

Block 210

Four of block 210 set together, as shown in the "Gallery of Four-Inch Blocks"

Two other designs created by changing block position

Note that several block designs can be used to create paper-pieced borders by joining them end to end.

Block 245 used as a border

Each foundation pattern is accompanied by a cutting list. The icons used in those lists are explained below.

Cutting List Icons

◹ = Cut each square into two half-square triangles.

⊠ = Cut each square into four quarter-square triangles.

A = Appliqué

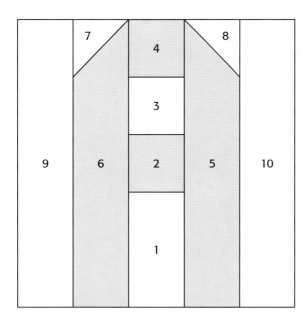

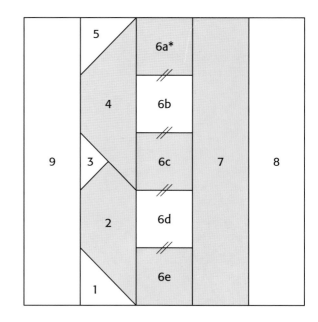

Block 1 Cutting List

Location	Size to Cut
7, 8	2" x 2" ◻
5, 6, 9, 10	1¼" x 3¾"
1	1¼" x 1¾"
2, 3, 4	1¼" x 1¼"

Block 2 Cutting List

Location	Size to Cut
1, 3, 5	2" x 2" ◻
2, 4	2" x 2"
7, 8, 9	1¼" x 3¾"
6a, 6b, 6c, 6d, 6e	1¼" x 1¼"

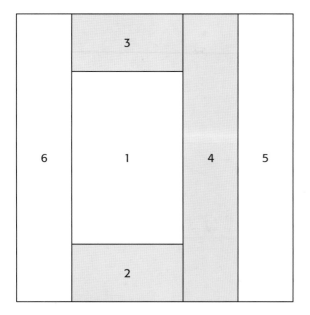

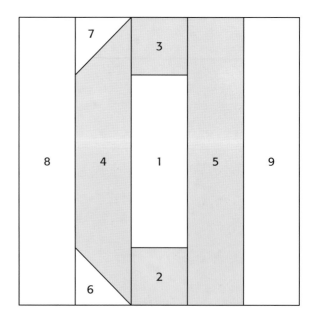

Block 3 Cutting List

Location	Size to Cut
1	2" x 2½"
4, 5, 6	1¼" x 3¾"
2, 3	1¼" x 2"

Block 4 Cutting List

Location	Size to Cut
6, 7	2" x 2" ◻
4, 5, 8, 9	1¼" x 3¾"
1	1¼" x 2½"
2, 3	1¼" x 1¼"

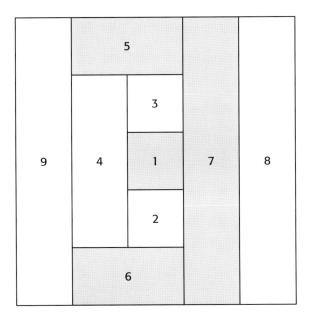

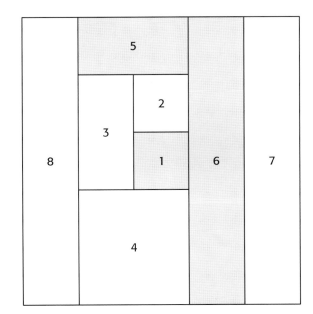

Block 5 Cutting List

Location	Size to Cut
7, 8, 9	1¼" x 3¾"
4	1¼" x 2½"
5, 6	1¼" x 2"
1, 2, 3	1¼" x 1¼"

Block 6 Cutting List

Location	Size to Cut
4	2" x 2"
6, 7, 8	1¼" x 3¾"
3, 5	1¼" x 2"
1, 2	1¼" x 1¼"

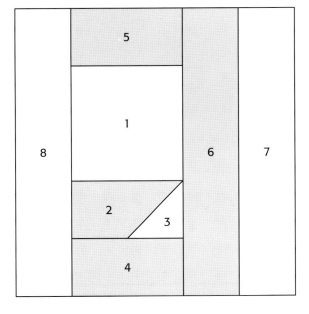

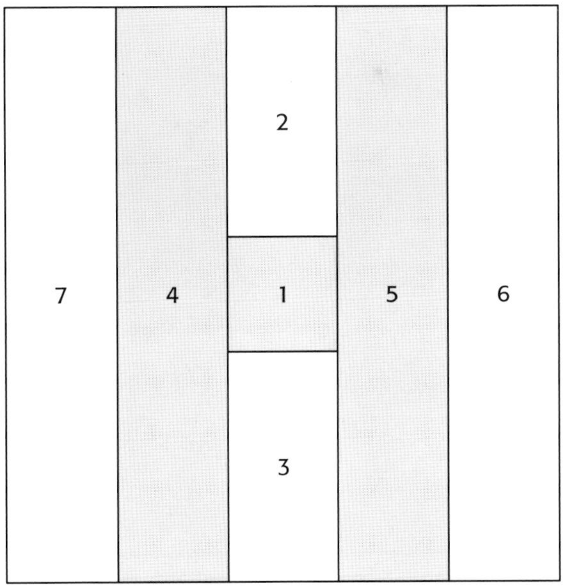

Block 7 Cutting List

Location	Size to Cut
1	2" x 2"
3	2" x 2" ◺
6, 7, 8	1¼" x 3¾"
2, 4, 5	1¼" x 2"

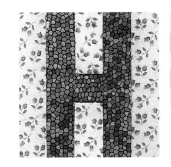

Block 8 Cutting List

Location	Size to Cut
4, 5, 6, 7	1¼" x 3¾"
2, 3	1¼" x 2"
1	1¼" x 1¼"

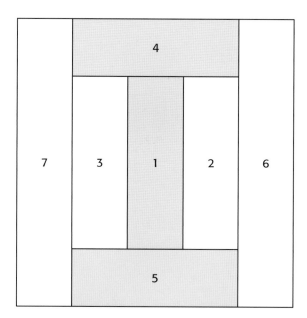

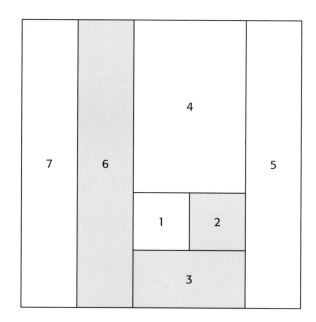

Block 9 Cutting List

Location	Size to Cut
6, 7	1¼" x 3¾"
1, 2, 3, 4, 5	1¼" x 2½"

Block 10 Cutting List

Location	Size to Cut
4	2" x 2½"
5, 6, 7	1¼" x 3¾"
3	1¼" x 2"
1, 2	1¼" x 1¼"

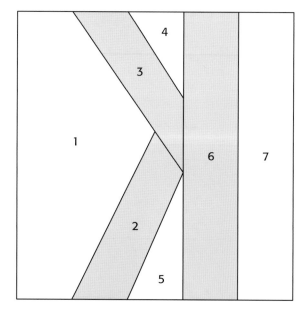

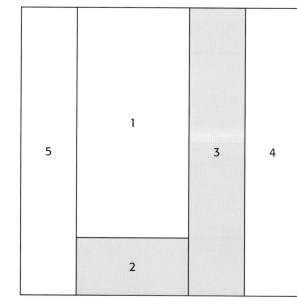

Block 11 Cutting List

Location	Size to Cut
1	2¼" x 3¾"
6, 7	1¼" x 3¾"
2, 3	1¼" x 3"
4, 5	1¼" x 2¼"

Block 12 Cutting List

Location	Size to Cut
1	2" x 3"
3, 4, 5	1¼" x 3¾"
2	1¼" x 2"

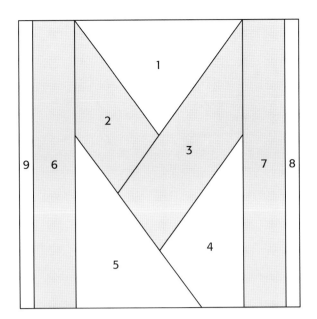

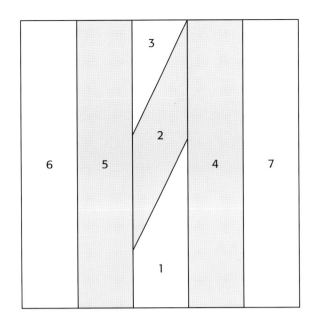

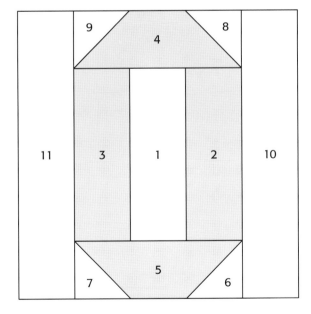

Block 13 Cutting List

Location	Size to Cut
1	2" x 2½"
4, 5	1¾" x 3"
2, 3	1½" x 3½"
6, 7, 8, 9	1¼" x 3¾"

Block 14 Cutting List

Location	Size to Cut
4, 5, 6, 7	1¼" x 3¾"
1, 3	1¼" x 2½"
2	1¼" x 3¼"

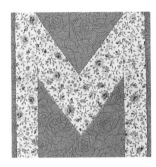

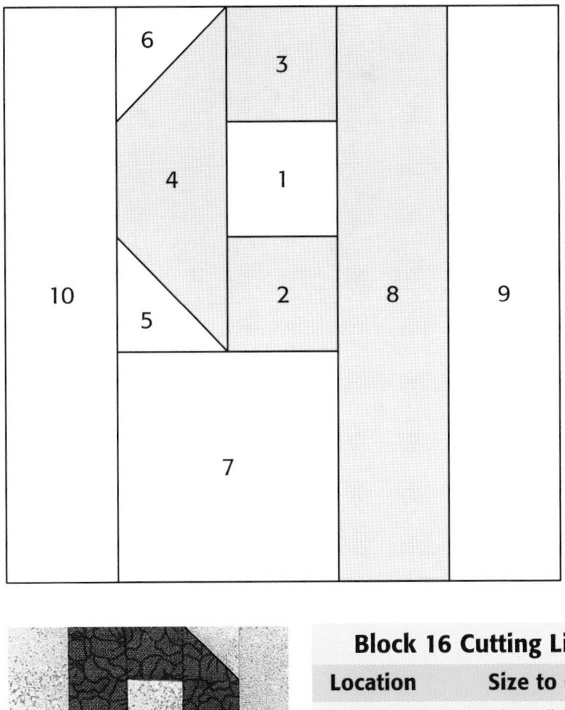

Block 15 Cutting List

Location	Size to Cut
6, 7, 8, 9	2" x 2" ◺
10, 11	1¼" x 3¾"
1, 2, 3, 4, 5	1¼" x 2½"

Block 16 Cutting List

Location	Size to Cut
7	2" x 2"
5, 6	2" x 2" ◺
4, 8, 9, 10	1¼" x 3¾"
1, 2, 3	1¼" x 1¼"

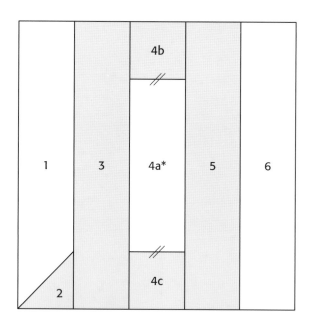

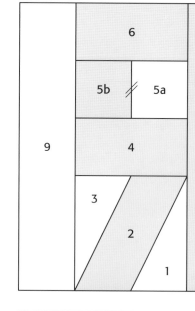

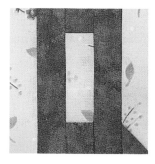

Block 17 Cutting List

Location	Size to Cut
2	2" x 2" ◻
1, 3, 5, 6	1¼" x 3¾"
4a	1¼" x 2½"
4b, 4c	1¼" x 1¼"

Block 18 Cutting List

Location	Size to Cut
7, 8, 9	1¼" x 3¾"
1, 2, 3	1¼" x 2½"
4, 6	1¼" x 2"
5a, 5b	1¼" x 1¼"

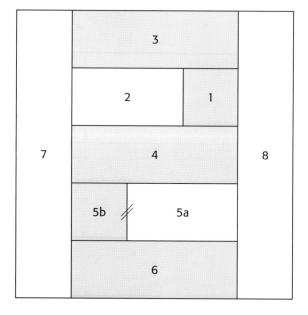

Block 19 Cutting List

Location	Size to Cut
7, 8	1¼" x 3¾"
3, 4, 6	1¼" x 2½"
1, 5a	1¼" x 2"
2, 5b	1¼" x 1¼"

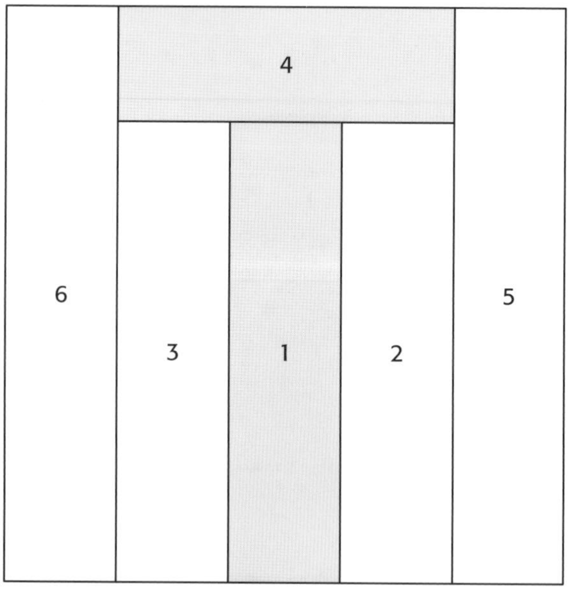

Block 20 Cutting List

Location	Size to Cut
5, 6	1¼" x 3¾"
1, 2, 3	1¼" x 3"
4	1¼" x 2½"

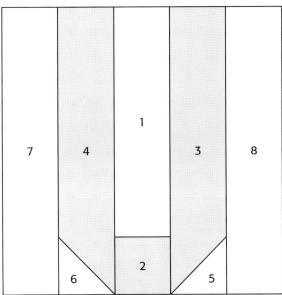

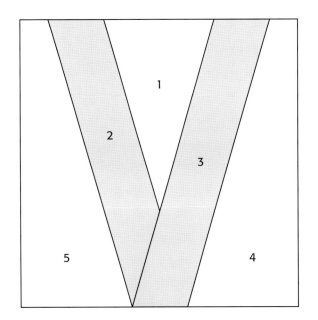

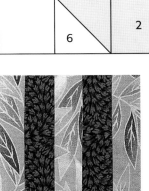

Block 21 Cutting List

Location	Size to Cut
5, 6	2" x 2" ◨
3, 4, 7, 8	1¼" x 3¾"
1	1¼" x 3"
2	1¼" x 1¼"

Block 22 Cutting List

Location	Size to Cut
4, 5	1¾" x 4"
1	1¾" x 2¾"
2, 3	1¼" x 4"

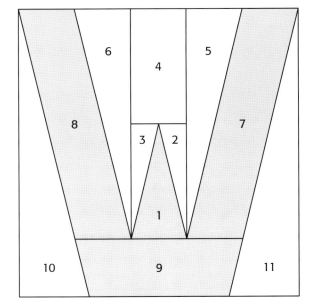

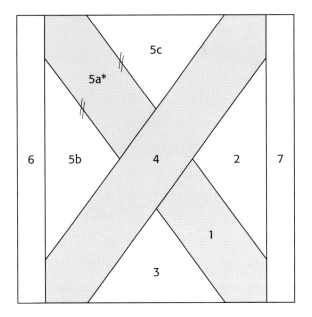

Block 23 Cutting List

Location	Size to Cut
10, 11	1½" x 3¾"
5, 6, 7, 8	1¼" x 3¼"
1, 4, 9	1¼" x 2½"
2, 3	1" x 2"

Block 24 Cutting List

Location	Size to Cut
2, 5b	2" x 2½"
3, 5c	2" x 2"
4, 6, 7	1¼" x 4½"
1, 5a	1¼" x 2½"

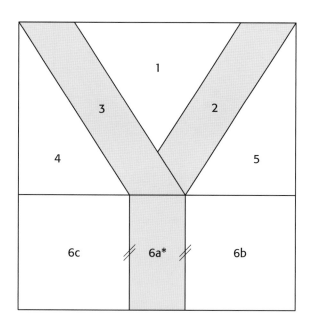

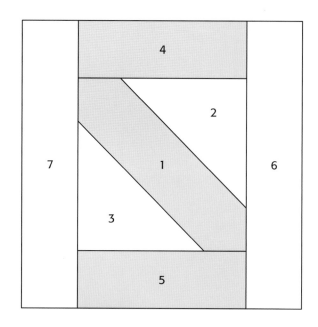

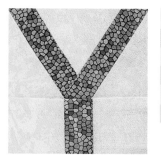

Block 25 Cutting List

Location	Size to Cut
1	2" x 2½"
4, 5, 6b, 6c	1¾" x 3"
2, 3	1¼" x 3¼"
6a	1¼" x 1¾"

Block 26 Cutting List

Location	Size to Cut
2, 3	2¾" x 2¾" ◨
1	1¼" x 3¼"
6, 7	1¼" x 3¾"
4, 5	1¼" x 2½"

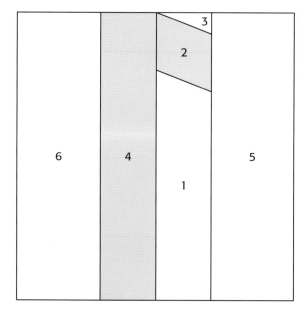

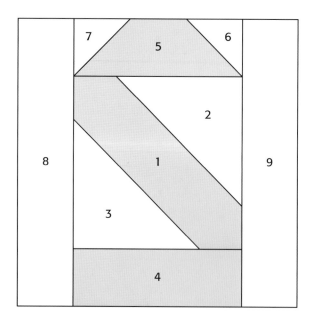

Block 27 Cutting List

Location	Size to Cut
4, 5, 6	1½" x 3¾"
1	1¼" x 3"
2	1¼" x 1½"
3	1¼" x 1"

Block 28 Cutting List

Location	Size to Cut
2, 3	2¾" x 2¾" ◨
6, 7	2" x 2" ◨
1, 8, 9	1¼" x 3¾"
4, 5	1¼" x 2½"

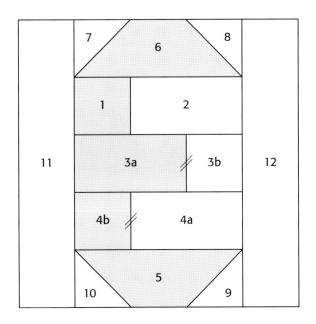

Block 29 Cutting List

Location	Size to Cut
7, 8, 9, 10	2" x 2" ◻
11, 12	1¼" x 3¾"
2, 3a, 4a, 5, 6	1¼" x 2½"
1, 3b, 4b	1¼" x 1¼"

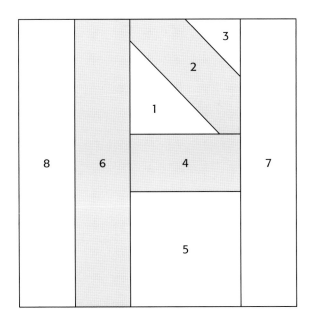

Block 30 Cutting List

Location	Size to Cut
1, 3	2¼" x 2¼" ◻
5	2" x 2"
6, 7, 8	1¼" x 3¾"
2, 4	1¼" x 2½"

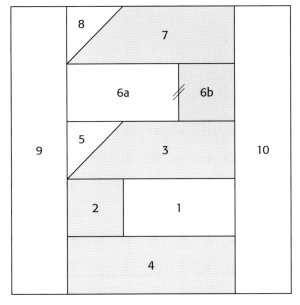

Block 31 Cutting List

Location	Size to Cut
5, 8	2" x 2" ◻
9, 10	1¼" x 3¾"
1, 3, 4, 6a, 7	1¼" x 2½"
2, 6b	1¼" x 1¼"

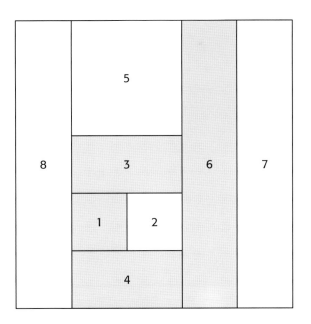

Block 32 Cutting List

Location	Size to Cut
5	2" x 2"
6, 7, 8	1¼" x 3¾"
3, 4	1¼" x 2"
1, 2	1¼" x 1¼"

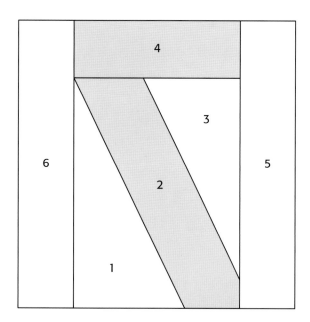

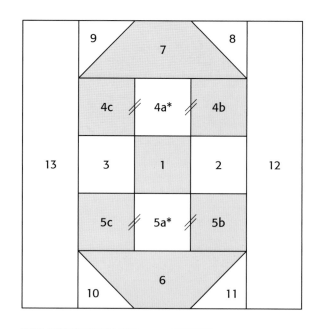

Block 33 Cutting List

Location	Size to Cut
1	2" x 3¼"
3	1¾" x 3"
2, 5, 6	1¼" x 4"
4	1¼" x 2½"

Block 34 Cutting List

Location	Size to Cut
8, 9, 10, 11	2" x 2" ◺
12, 13	1¼" x 3¾"
6, 7	1¼" x 2½"
1, 2, 3, 4a, 4b, 4c, 5a, 5b, 5c	1¼" x 1¼"

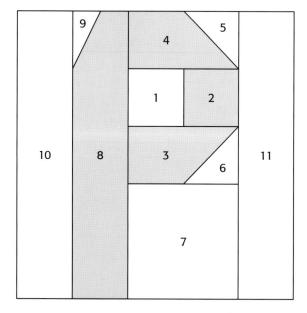

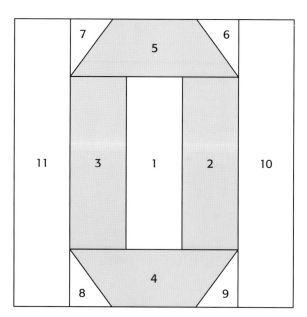

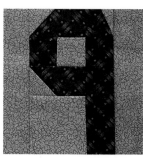

Block 35 Cutting List

Location	Size to Cut
7	2" x 2"
5, 6	2" x 2" ◺
8, 10, 11	1¼" x 3¾"
1, 2, 3, 4, 9	1¼" x 2"

Block 36 Cutting List

Location	Size to Cut
6, 7, 8, 9	2" x 2" ◺
10, 11	1¼" x 3¾"
1, 2, 3, 4, 5	1¼" x 2½"

GALLERY OF FOUR-INCH BLOCKS

This gallery shows the 4" blocks in four-block groups.

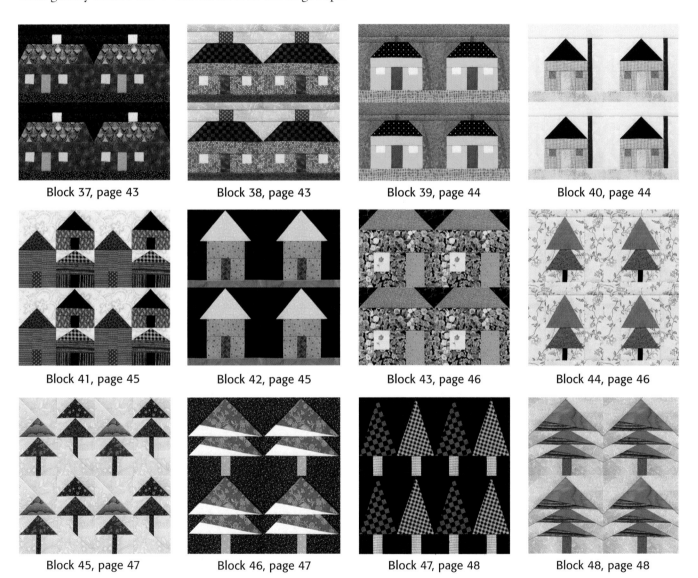

Block 37, page 43

Block 38, page 43

Block 39, page 44

Block 40, page 44

Block 41, page 45

Block 42, page 45

Block 43, page 46

Block 44, page 46

Block 45, page 47

Block 46, page 47

Block 47, page 48

Block 48, page 48

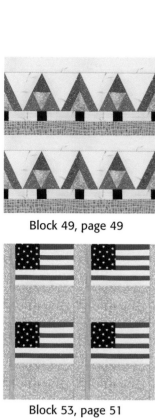

Block 49, page 49

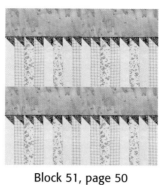

Block 50, page 49

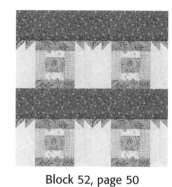

Block 51, page 50

Block 52, page 50

Block 53, page 51

Block 54, page 51

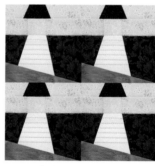

Block 55, page 52

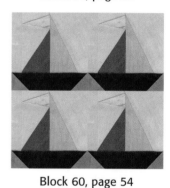

Block 56, page 52

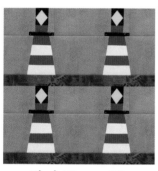

Block 57, page 53

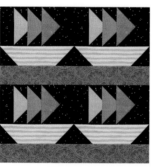

Block 58, page 53

Block 59, page 54

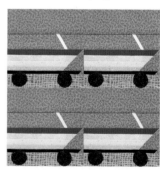

Block 60, page 54

Block 61, page 55

Block 62, page 55

Block 63, page 56

Block 64, page 56

Block 65, page 57

Block 66, page 57

Block 67, page 58

Block 68, page 58

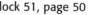

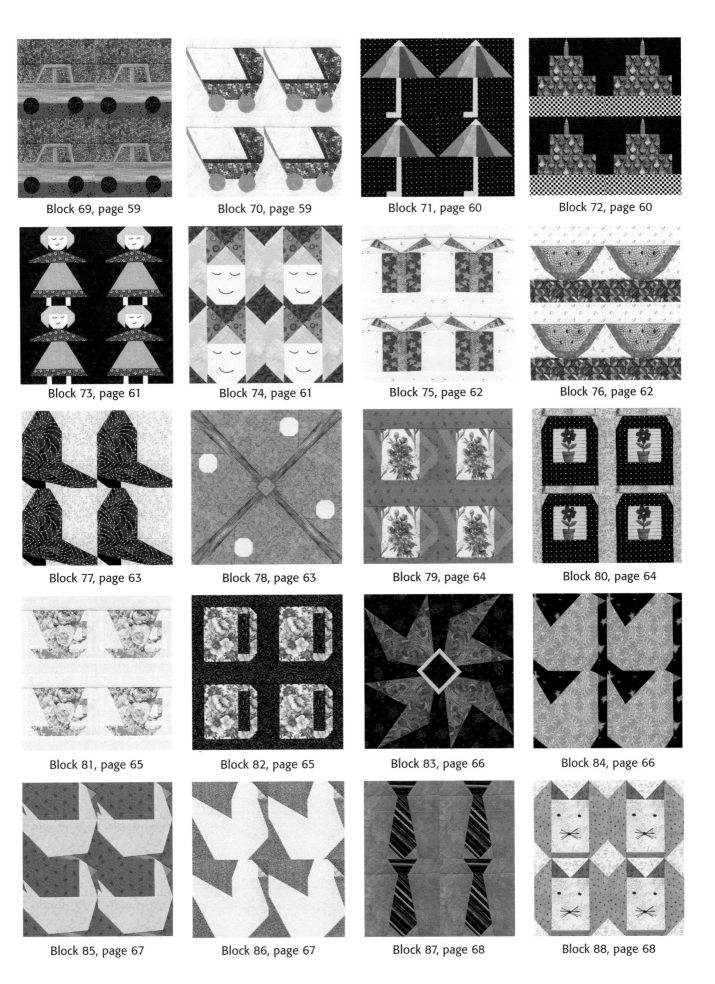

Block 69, page 59

Block 70, page 59

Block 71, page 60

Block 72, page 60

Block 73, page 61

Block 74, page 61

Block 75, page 62

Block 76, page 62

Block 77, page 63

Block 78, page 63

Block 79, page 64

Block 80, page 64

Block 81, page 65

Block 82, page 65

Block 83, page 66

Block 84, page 66

Block 85, page 67

Block 86, page 67

Block 87, page 68

Block 88, page 68

Block 89, page 69

Block 90, page 69

Block 91, page 70

Block 92, page 70

Block 93, page 71

Block 94, page 71

Block 95, page 72

Block 96, page 72

Block 97, page 73

Block 98, page 73

Block 99, page 74

Block 100, page 74

Block 101, page 75

Block 102, page 75

Block 103, page 76

Block 104, page 76

Block 105, page 77

Block 106, page 77

Block 107, page 78

Block 108, page 78

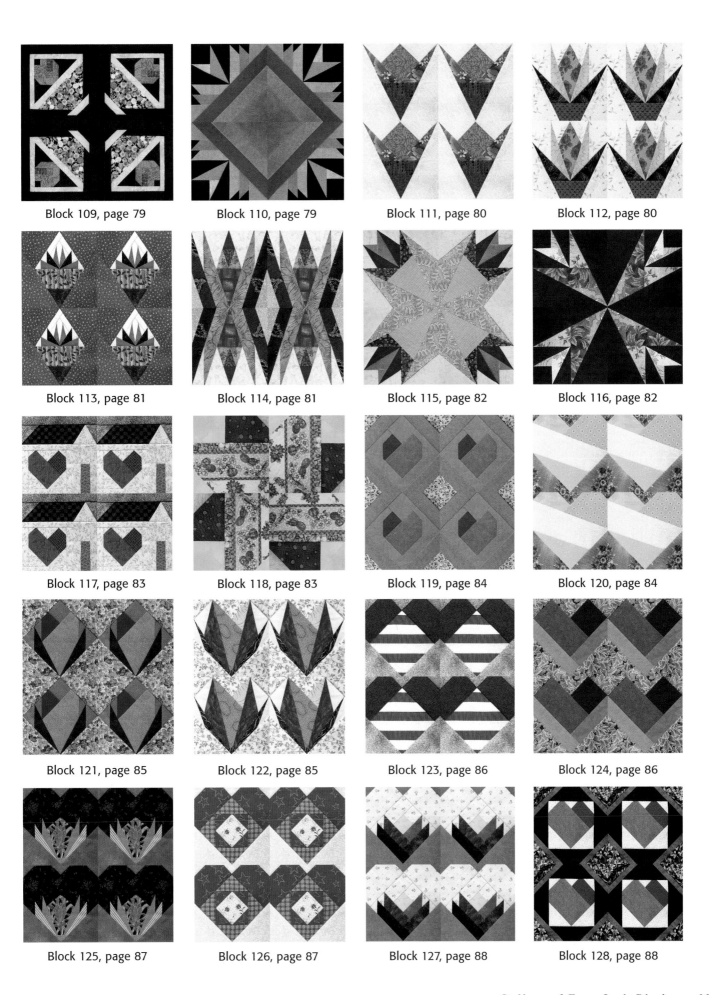

Block 109, page 79   Block 110, page 79   Block 111, page 80   Block 112, page 80

Block 113, page 81   Block 114, page 81   Block 115, page 82   Block 116, page 82

Block 117, page 83   Block 118, page 83   Block 119, page 84   Block 120, page 84

Block 121, page 85   Block 122, page 85   Block 123, page 86   Block 124, page 86

Block 125, page 87   Block 126, page 87   Block 127, page 88   Block 128, page 88

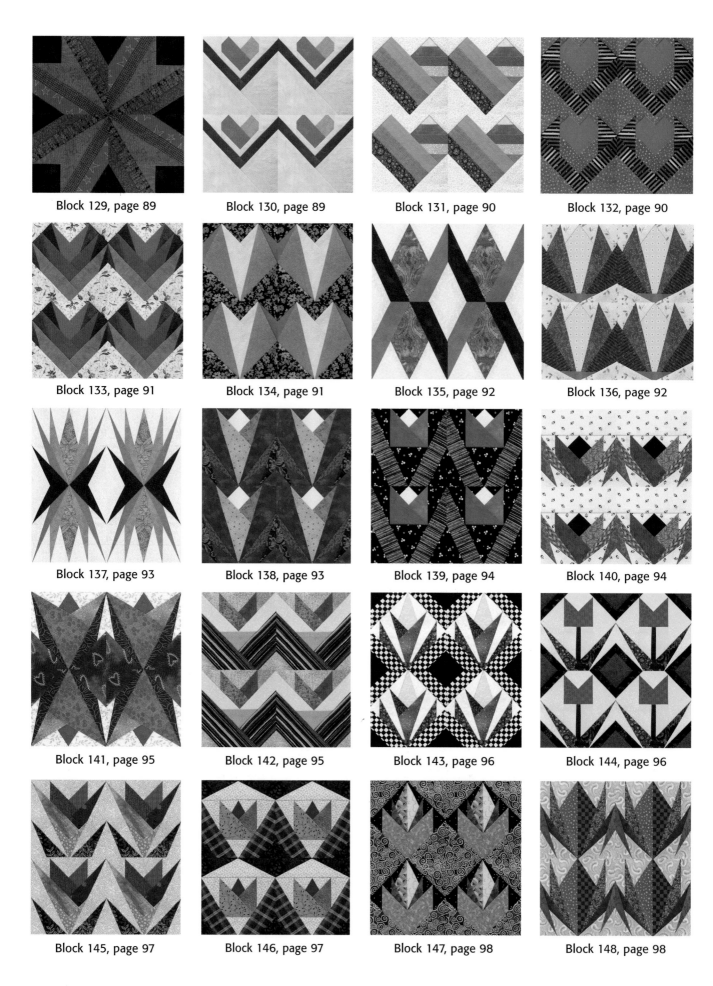

Block 129, page 89

Block 130, page 89

Block 131, page 90

Block 132, page 90

Block 133, page 91

Block 134, page 91

Block 135, page 92

Block 136, page 92

Block 137, page 93

Block 138, page 93

Block 139, page 94

Block 140, page 94

Block 141, page 95

Block 142, page 95

Block 143, page 96

Block 144, page 96

Block 145, page 97

Block 146, page 97

Block 147, page 98

Block 148, page 98

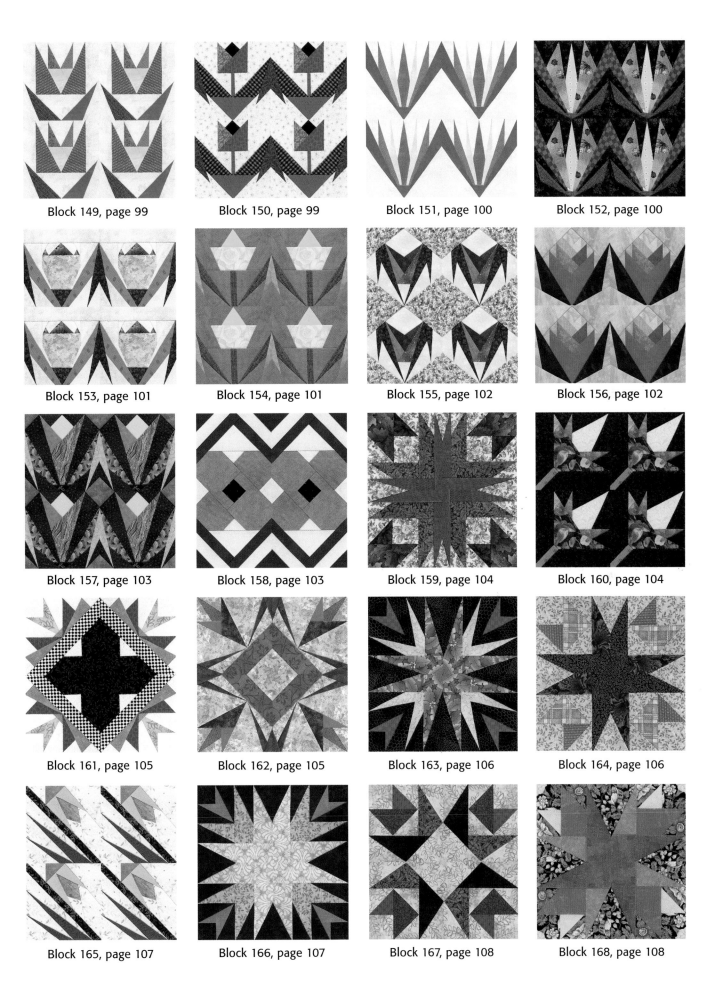

Block 149, page 99

Block 150, page 99

Block 151, page 100

Block 152, page 100

Block 153, page 101

Block 154, page 101

Block 155, page 102

Block 156, page 102

Block 157, page 103

Block 158, page 103

Block 159, page 104

Block 160, page 104

Block 161, page 105

Block 162, page 105

Block 163, page 106

Block 164, page 106

Block 165, page 107

Block 166, page 107

Block 167, page 108

Block 168, page 108

Block 169, page 109   Block 170, page 109   Block 171, page 110   Block 172, page 110

Block 173, page 111   Block 174, page 111   Block 175, page 112   Block 176, page 112

Block 177, page 113   Block 178, page 113   Block 179, page 114   Block 180, page 114

Block 181, page 115   Block 182, page 115   Block 183, page 116   Block 184, page 116

Block 185, page 117   Block 186, page 117   Block 187, page 118   Block 188, page 118

Block 189, page 119

Block 190, page 119

Block 191, page 120

Block 192, page 120

Block 193, page 121

Block 194, page 121

Block 195, page 122

Block 196, page 122

Block 197, page 123

Block 198, page 123

Block 199, page 124

Block 200, page 124

Block 201, page 125

Block 202, page 125

Block 203, page 126

Block 204, page 126

Block 205, page 127

Block 206, page 127

Block 207, page 128

Block 208, page 128

Block 209, page 129

Block 210, page 129

Block 211, page 130

Block 212, page 130

Block 213, page 131

Block 214, page 131

Block 215, page 132

Block 216, page 132

Block 217, page 133

Block 218, page 133

Block 219, page 134

Block 220, page 134

Block 221, page 135

Block 222, page 135

Block 223, page 136

Block 224, page 136

Block 225, page 137

Block 226, page 137

Block 227, page 138

Block 228, page 138

Block 229, page 139

Block 230, page 139

Block 231, page 140

Block 232, page 140

Block 233, page 141

Block 234, page 141

Block 235, page 142

Block 236, page 142

Block 237, page 143

Block 238, page 143

Block 239, page 144

Block 240, page 144

Block 241, page 145

Block 242, page 145

Block 243, page 146

Block 244, page 146

Block 245, page 147

Block 246, page 147

Block 247, page 148

Block 248, page 148

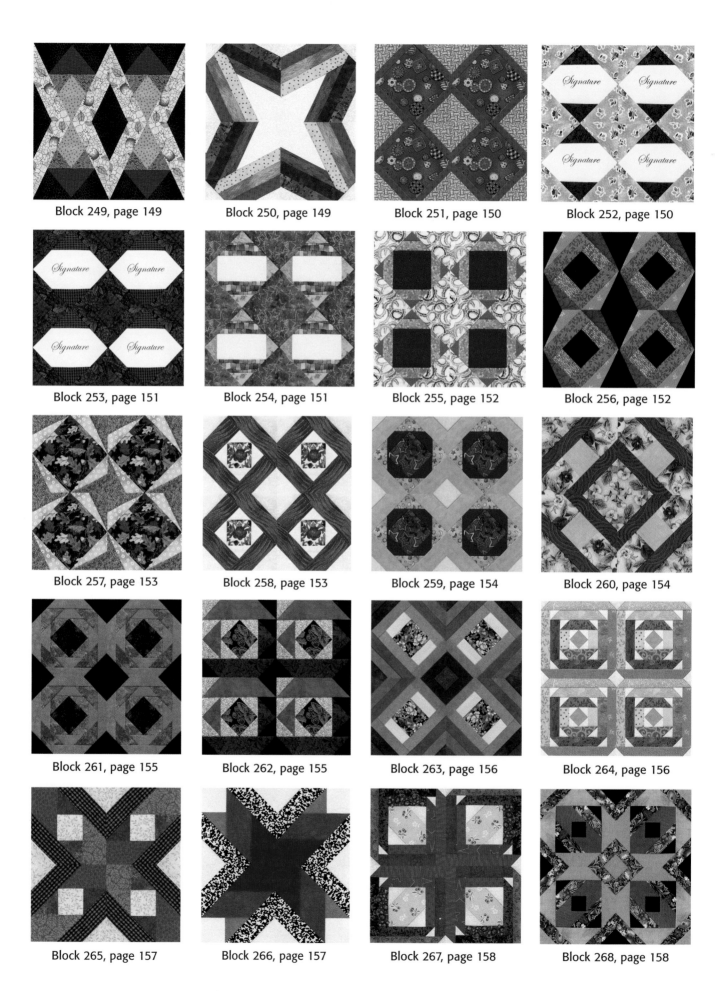

Block 249, page 149

Block 250, page 149

Block 251, page 150

Block 252, page 150

Block 253, page 151

Block 254, page 151

Block 255, page 152

Block 256, page 152

Block 257, page 153

Block 258, page 153

Block 259, page 154

Block 260, page 154

Block 261, page 155

Block 262, page 155

Block 263, page 156

Block 264, page 156

Block 265, page 157

Block 266, page 157

Block 267, page 158

Block 268, page 158

Block 269, page 159

Block 270, page 159

Block 271, page 160

Block 272, page 160

Block 273, page 161

Block 274, page 161

Block 275, page 162

Block 276, page 162

Block 277, page 163

Block 278, page 163

Block 279, page 164

Block 280, page 164

Block 281, page 165

Block 282, page 165

Block 283, page 166

Block 284, page 166

Block 285, page 167

Block 286, page 167

Block 287, page 168

Block 288, page 168

Block 289, page 169   Block 290, page 169   Block 291, page 170   Block 292, page 170

Block 293, page 171   Block 294, page 171   Block 295, page 172   Block 296, page 172

Block 297, page 173   Block 298, page 173   Block 299, page 174   Block 300, page 174

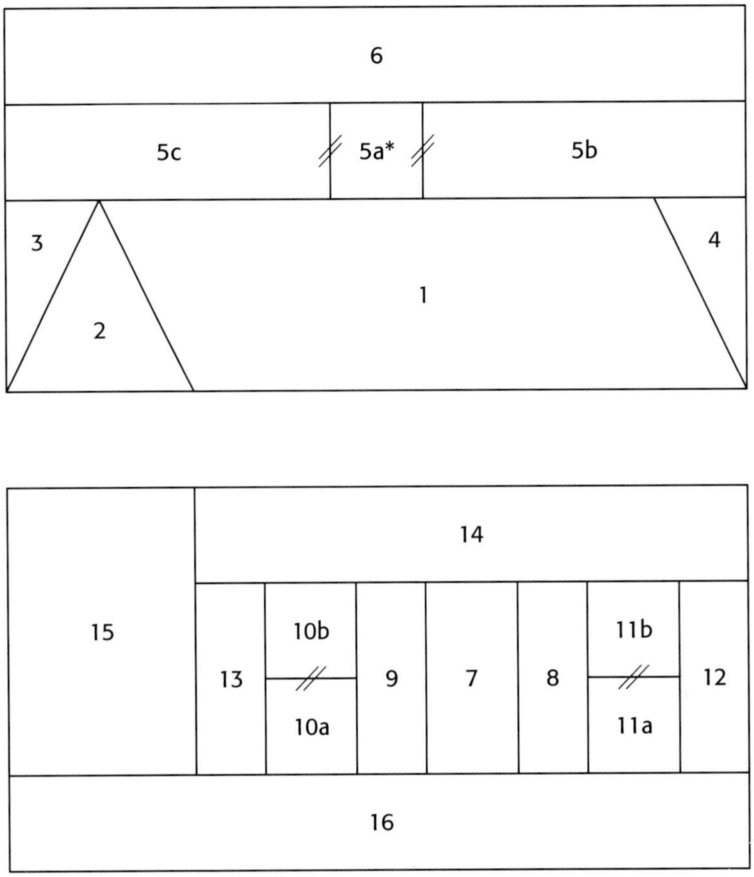

FOUR-INCH BLOCKS

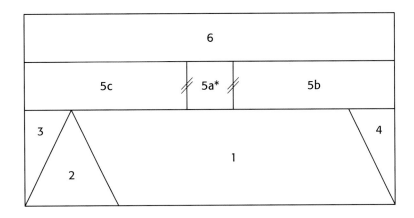

37

Block 37 Cutting List

Location	Size to Cut
1	1¾" x 4¼"
2, 15	1½" x 2¼"
6, 14, 16	1¼" x 4¾"
5b, 5c	1¼" x 2½"
7, 8, 9, 12, 13	1¼" x 1½"
10a, 10b, 11a, 11b	1¼" x 1¼"
3, 4	1" x 1¾"
5a	1" x 1¼"

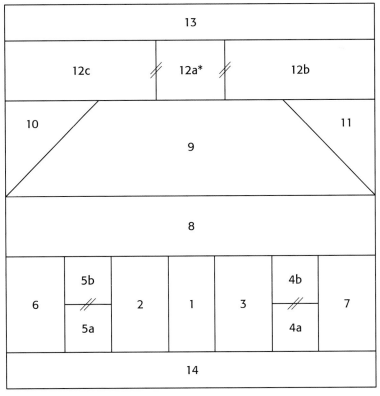

38

Block 38 Cutting List

Location	Size to Cut
10, 11	2¼" x 2¼" ◻
9	1¾" x 4¾"
8, 13, 14	1¼" x 4¾"
12b, 12c	1¼" x 2¼"
1, 2, 3, 6, 7	1¼" x 1¾"
4a, 4b, 5a, 5b, 12a	1¼" x 1¼"

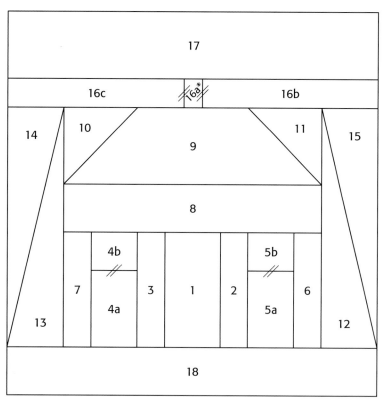

39

Block 39 Cutting List

Location	Size to Cut
10, 11	2" x 2" ◺
17, 18	1½" x 4¾"
8, 9, 12, 13, 14, 15	1¼" x 3½"
1	1¼" x 1¾"
16b, 16c	1" x 2½"
2, 3, 4a, 5a, 6, 7	1" x 1¾"
4b, 5b, 16a	1" x 1"

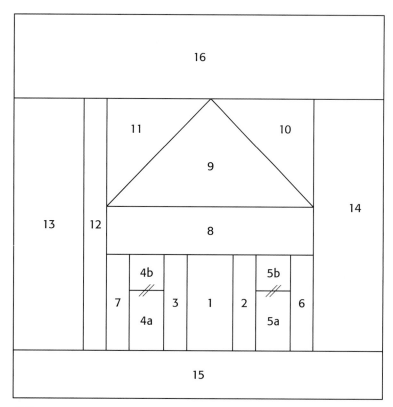

40

Block 40 Cutting List

Location	Size to Cut
10, 11	2½" x 2½" ◺
9	1¾" x 3"
16	1½" x 4¾"
13, 14	1½" x 3¼"
15	1¼" x 4¾"
8	1¼" x 3"
1, 2, 3, 4a, 4b, 5a, 5b, 6, 7	1¼" x 1½"
12	1" x 3¼"

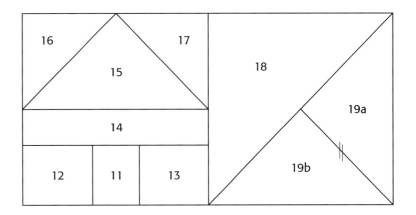

Block 41 Cutting List

Location	Size to Cut
15, 19a, 19b	3½" x 3½" ⊠
18	3¼" x 3¼" ◹
16, 17	2¼" x 2¼" ◹
4, 5, 6, 7, 8, 10, 14	1½" x 2¾"
1, 2, 3, 11, 12, 13	1½" x 1½"
9a, 9b	1¼" x 1¾"

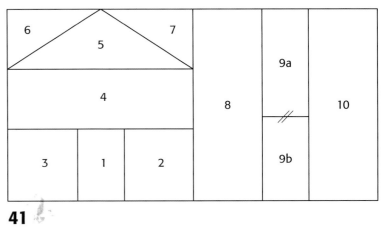

41

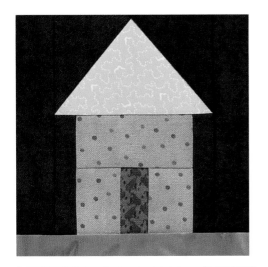

Block 42 Cutting List

Location	Size to Cut
8, 9	3" x 3" ◹
7	2½" x 3½"
4	1½" x 2¾"
2, 3	1½" x 1¾"
10, 11, 12	1¼" x 4¾"
1	1¼" x 1¾"
5, 6	1" x 2¾"

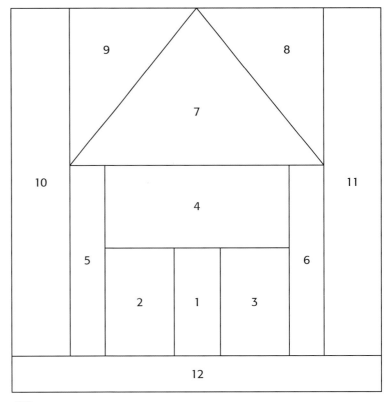

42

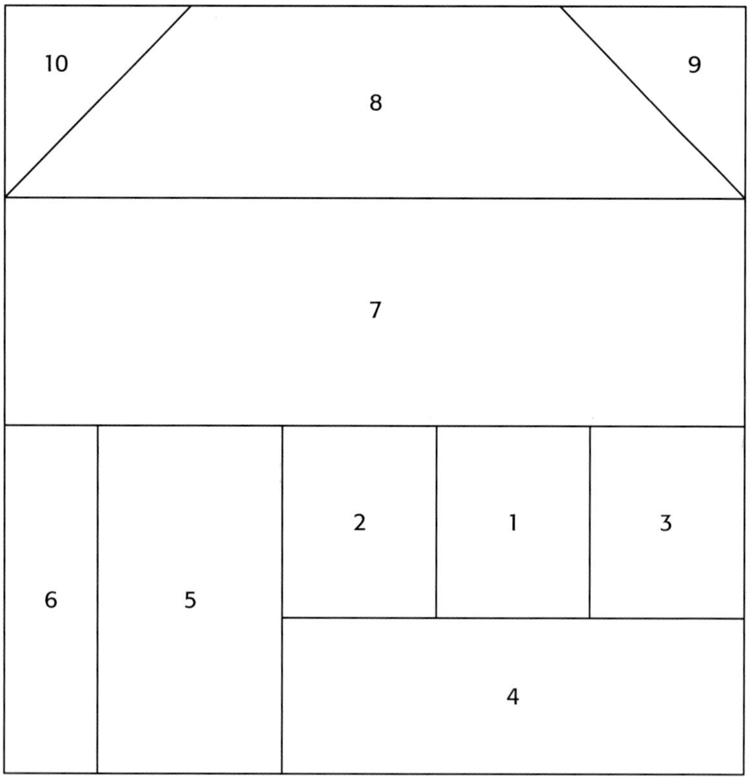

43

Block 43 Cutting List

Location	Size to Cut
9, 10	2¼" x 2¼" ◺
7, 8	1¾" x 4¾"
5	1¾" x 2½"
4	1½" x 3¼"
1, 2, 3	1½" x 1½"
6	1¼" x 2½"

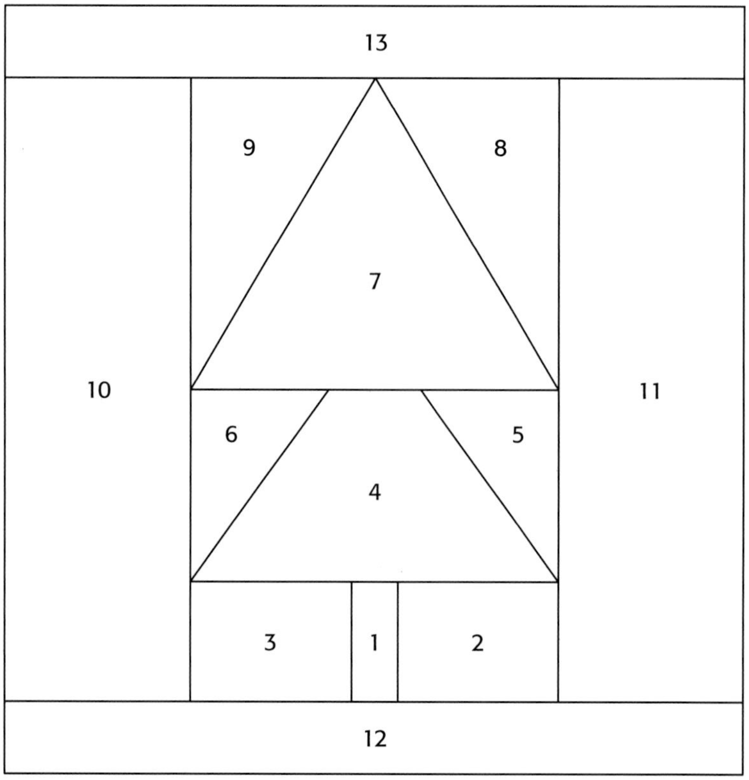

44

Block 44 Cutting List

Location	Size to Cut
7	2¼" x 2¾"
4	1¾" x 2¾"
10, 11	1½" x 4"
8, 9	1½" x 2¾"
5, 6	1¼" x 2"
1, 2, 3	1¼" x 1¼"
12, 13	1" x 4¾"

Block 45 Cutting List

Location	Size to Cut
4, 7, 14, 17, 18	3½" x 3½" ⊠
10, 19	3¼" x 3¼" ◺
2, 5, 6, 8, 9, 15, 16	2¼" x 2¼" ◺
3	1½" x 2¾"
12, 13	1½" x 1¾"
1, 11	1" x 1¾"

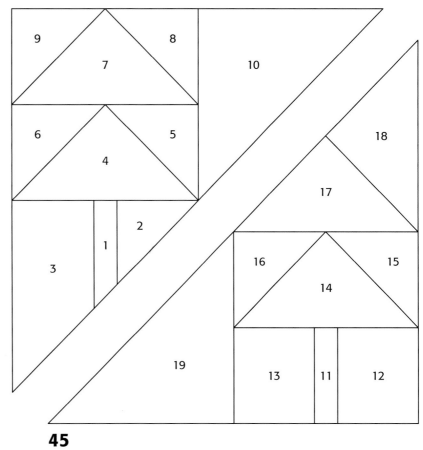

45

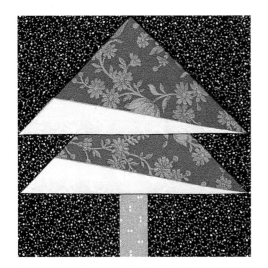

Block 46 Cutting List

Location	Size to Cut
10, 11	3¼" x 3¼" ◺
9	2¼" x 4¼"
6, 7	2¼" x 2¼" ◺
2, 3	1¾" x 2½"
5	1½" x 4¼"
4, 8	1¼" x 4¾"
1	1¼" x 1¾"

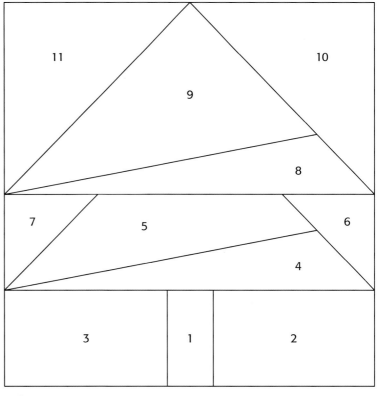

46

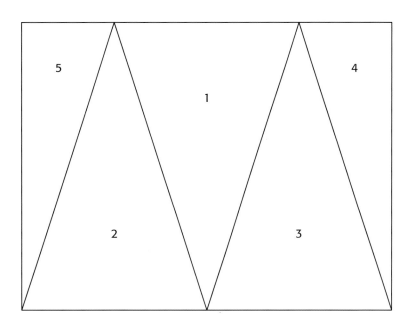

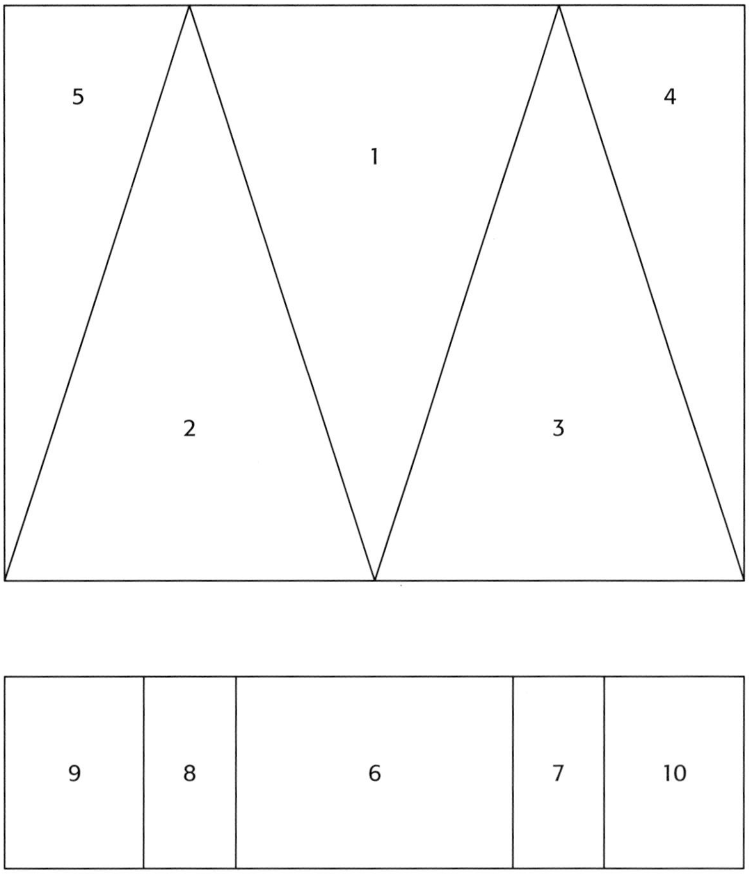

Block 47 Cutting List

Location	Size to Cut
1	2¾" x 3¾"
2, 3	2½" x 4"
6	1¾" x 2¼"
4, 5	1½" x 4"
7, 8, 9, 10	1½" x 1¾"

47

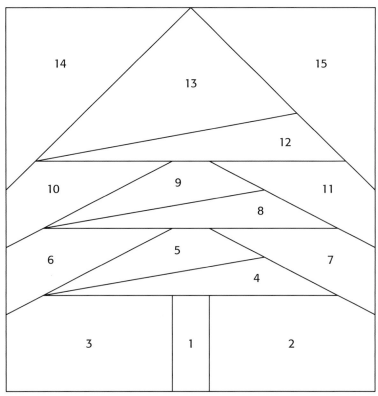

Block 48 Cutting List

Location	Size to Cut
14, 15	3¼" x 3¼" ◪
13	2" x 3¾"
2, 3	1¾" x 2½"
4, 5, 8, 9, 12	1¼" x 4"
6, 7, 10, 11	1¼" x 2¾"
1	1¼" x 1¾"

48

Block 49 Cutting List

Location	Size to Cut
5, 6	2½" x 3"
1, 2, 3, 4	1¾" x 1¾"
12, 13	1½" x 4¾"
11a, 11b	1¼" x 2"
7, 8, 9, 10	1" x 3"
11c, 11d, 11e	1" x 1¼"

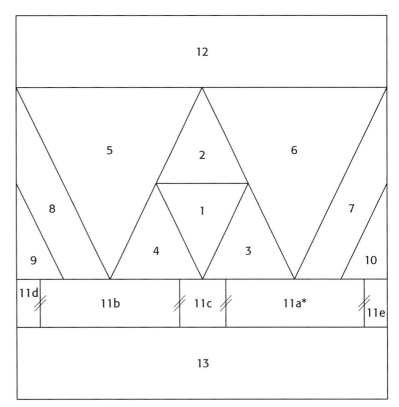

49

Block 50 Cutting List

Location	Size to Cut
8	2" x 4¾"
1, 2, 3, 4, 5	1¼" x 3¾"
6, 7	1¼" x 3½"

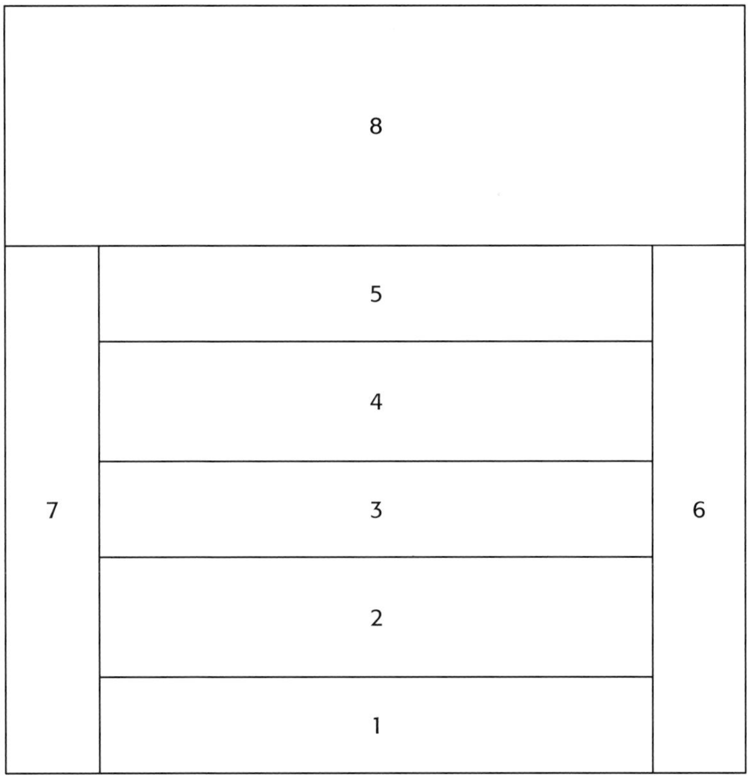

50

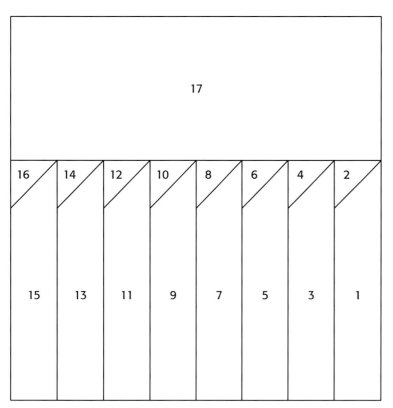

51

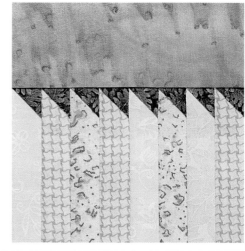

Block 51 Cutting List	
Location	**Size to Cut**
17	2¼" x 4¾"
2, 4, 6, 8, 10, 12, 14, 16	1¾" x 1¾" ◪
1, 3, 5, 7, 9, 11, 13, 15	1¼" x 3¼"

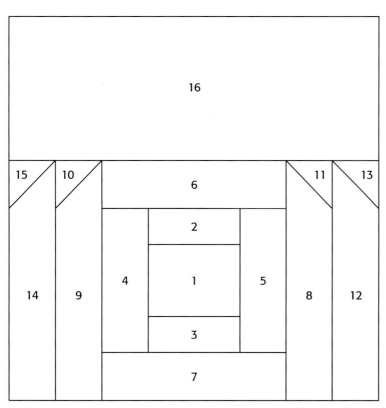

52

Block 52 Cutting List	
Location	**Size to Cut**
16	2¼" x 4¾"
10, 11, 13, 15	1¾" x 1¾" ◪
1, 2, 3	1½" x 1¾"
8, 9, 12, 14	1¼" x 3¼"
4, 5, 6, 7	1¼" x 2¾"

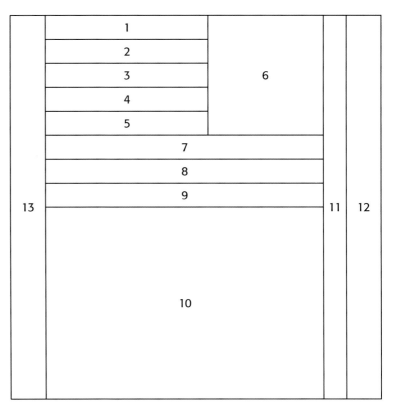

53

Block 53 Cutting List

Location	Size to Cut
10	2¾" x 3¾"
6	2" x 2"
11, 12, 13	1" x 4¾"
7, 8, 9	1" x 3½"
1, 2, 3, 4, 5	1" x 2½"

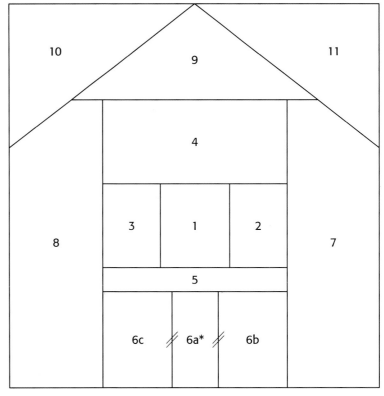

54

Block 54 Cutting List

Location	Size to Cut
10, 11	2" x 3¾"
7, 8, 9	1¾" x 3¾"
4	1½" x 2¾"
1, 2, 3, 6a, 6b, 6c	1½" x 1¾"
5	1" x 2¾"

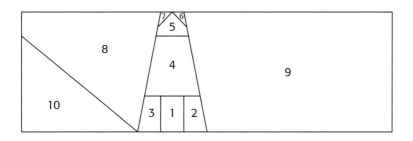

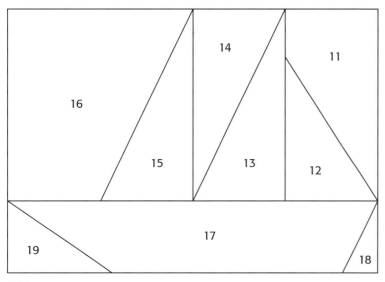

55

Block 55 Cutting List

Location	Size to Cut
16	2½" x 3½"
9	2½" x 3"
8	2" x 2¼"
10, 11, 12, 13, 14, 15	1¾" x 2¾"
17	1½" x 4¾"
18, 19	1¼" x 2½"
1, 2, 3, 4, 5, 6, 7	1¼" x 1¼"

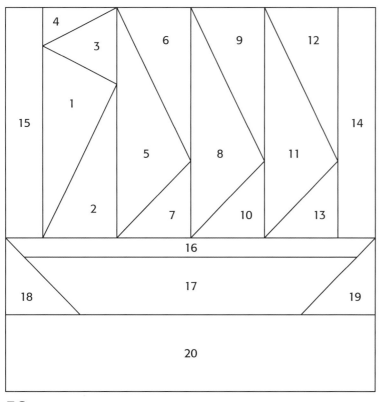

56

Block 56 Cutting List

Location	Size to Cut
7, 10, 13, 18, 19	2" x 2" ◻
16, 17, 20	1½" x 4¾"
5, 8, 11, 14, 15	1½" x 3¼"
1, 2, 6, 9, 12	1½" x 2¾"
3, 4	1¼" x 1¾"

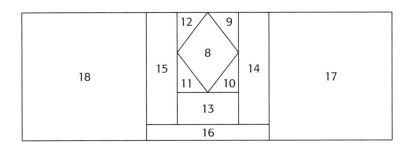

Block 57 Cutting List

Location	Size to Cut
5, 6	2¼" x 3"
17, 18	2" x 2"
9, 10, 11, 12	1¾" x 1¾" ◹
8	1½" x 1½"
7	1¼" x 4¾"
1, 2, 3, 4	1¼" x 2¼"
13, 14, 15, 16	1" x 2"

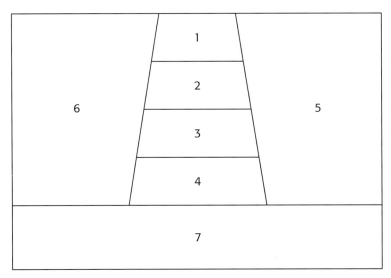

57

Block 58 Cutting List

Location	Size to Cut
8, 9, 13, 14	2¼" x 2¼" ◹
2, 3, 5, 6	2" x 2" ◹
12, 15	1¾" x 4¾"
1, 4, 7, 10, 11	1½" x 2¾"

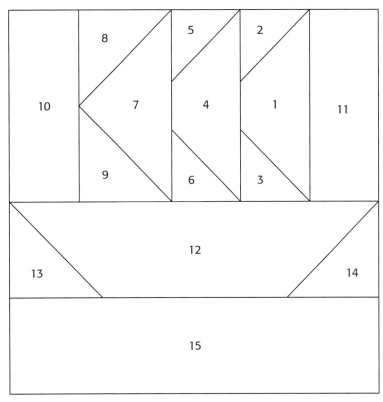

58

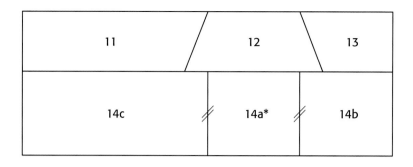

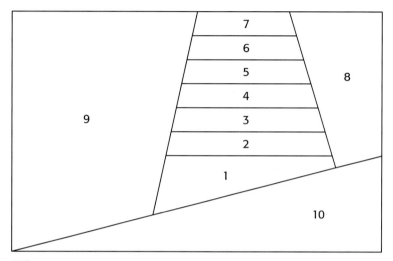

59

Block 59 Cutting List	
Location	**Size to Cut**
9	2½" x 3¾"
10	1¾" x 5"
8, 12, 13	1¾" x 2½"
1, 14b, 14c	1½" x 2¾"
14a	1½" x 1½"
11	1¼" x 2½"
2, 3, 4, 5, 6, 7	1" x 2"

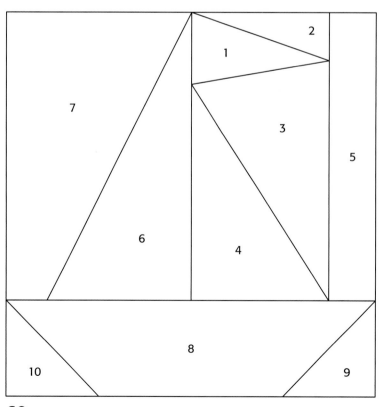

60

Block 60 Cutting List	
Location	**Size to Cut**
7	2½" x 4½"
3, 4, 6	2¼" x 3¾"
9, 10	2¼" x 2¼" ◻
8	1¾" x 4¾"
1, 2	1½" x 2½"
5	1¼" x 3¾"

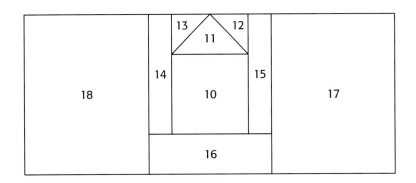

Block 61 Cutting List

Location	Size to Cut
7, 8	2" x 2¾"
17, 18	2" x 2¼"
12, 13	1¾" x 1¾" ◻
2, 3, 10	1½" x 1½"
9	1" x 4¾"
1, 4, 5, 6, 11, 14, 15, 16	1" x 2¼"

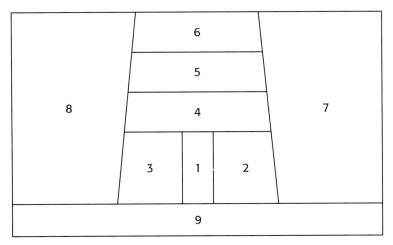

61

Block 62 Cutting List

Location	Size to Cut
2, 3	2½" x 3"
6	1¾" x 4¾"
1, 7, 8	1½" x 3"
4, 5, 9b, 9c	1¼" x 2¼"
9a	1¼" x 1½"

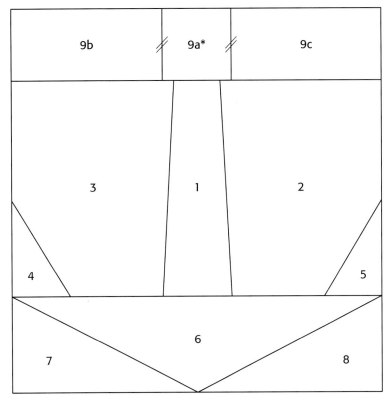

62

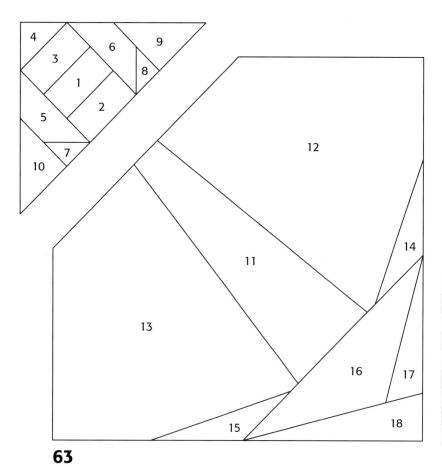

63

Block 63 Cutting List

Location	Size to Cut
12, 13	3" x 3¾"
9, 10	2¼" x 2¼" ◺
11	1¾" x 3½"
4, 7, 8	1¾" x 1¾" ◺
16	1½" x 4"
14, 15, 17, 18	1¼" x 3"
1, 2, 3, 5, 6	1" x 1¾"

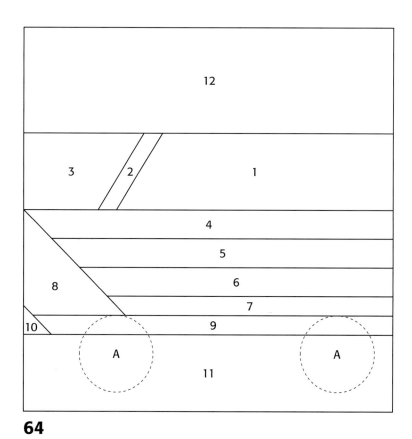

64

Block 64 Cutting List

Location	Size to Cut
3	2" x 2"
12	1¾" x 4¾"
1, 11	1½" x 4¾"
8	1½" x 2½"
4, 5, 6, 7, 9	1" x 4¾"
2, 10	1" x 2"

Block 65 Cutting List

Location	Size to Cut
8	2½" x 3"
7	1¾" x 3"
9, 10	1½" x 4¾"
1, 2, 3, 4, 5, 6	1½" x 2"

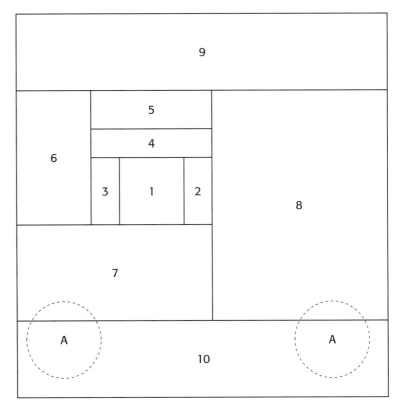

65

Block 66 Cutting List

Location	Size to Cut
7	2" x 2¾"
8	1¾" x 4¾"
9, 10	1½" x 4¾"
1, 2, 3, 4, 5, 6	1½" x 2"

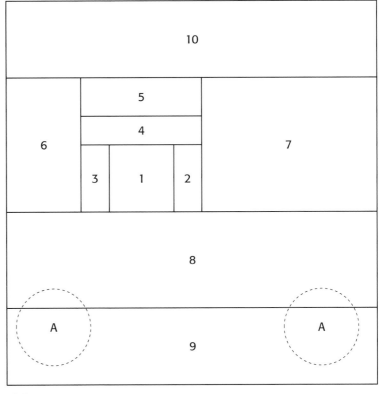

66

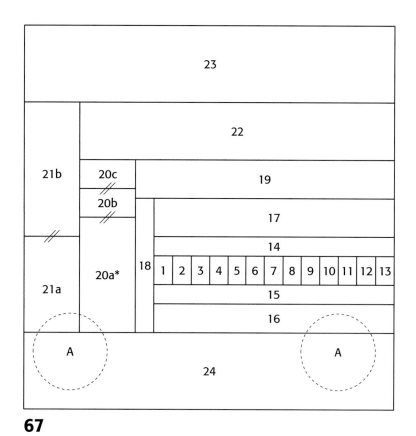

67

Block 67 Cutting List	
Location	**Size to Cut**
23, 24	1½" x 4¾"
22	1¼" x 4¼"
20a, 21a, 21b	1¼" x 2"
14, 15, 16, 17, 18, 19	1" x 3¾"
20b, 20c	1" x 1¼"
1, 2, 3, 4, 5, 6, 7, 8, 9, 10, 11, 12, 13	1" x 1"

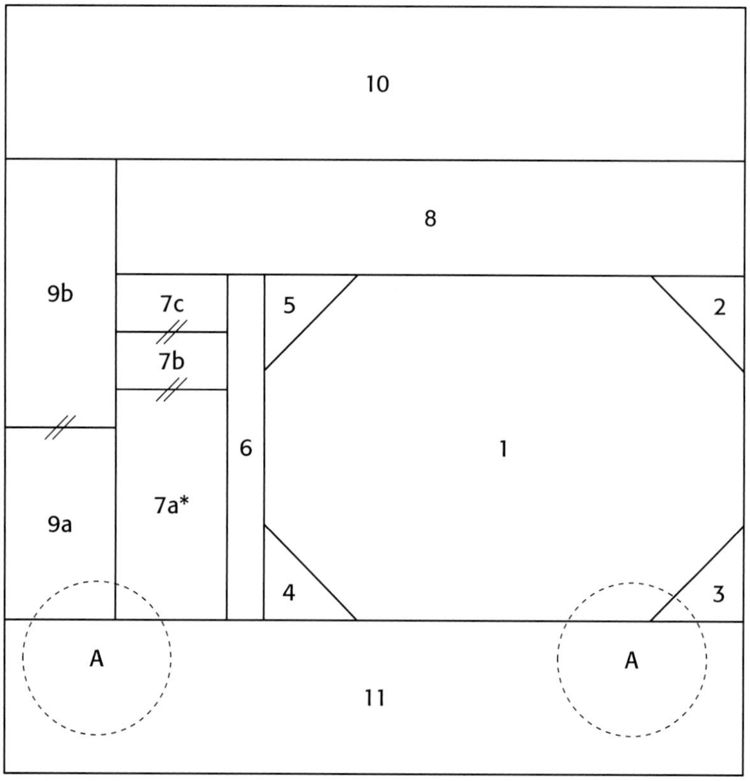

68

Block 68 Cutting List	
Location	**Size to Cut**
1	2½" x 3½"
2, 3, 4, 5	1¾" x 1¾" ◻
10, 11	1½" x 4¾"
8	1¼" x 4¼"
7a, 9a, 9b	1¼" x 2"
7b, 7c	1¼" x 1¼"
6	1" x 2½"

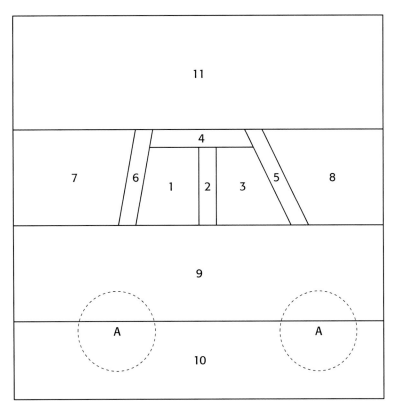

Block 69 Cutting List

Location	Size to Cut
11	2" x 4¾"
1, 3, 7, 8	2" x 2"
9, 10	1¾" x 4¾"
2, 4, 5, 6	1" x 2"

69

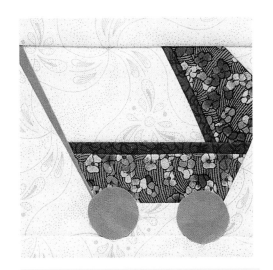

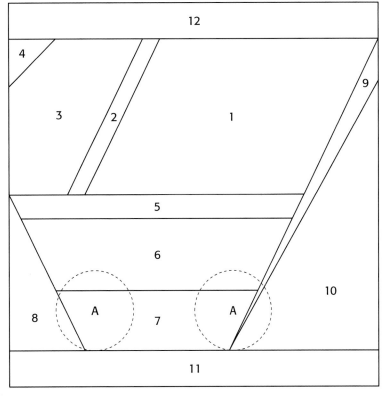

Block 70 Cutting List

Location	Size to Cut
1, 10	2¼" x 4"
3	2" x 2¾"
6	1½" x 3¾"
2, 7, 8	1¼" x 3"
5, 9, 11, 12	1" x 4¾"
4	1" x 2"

70

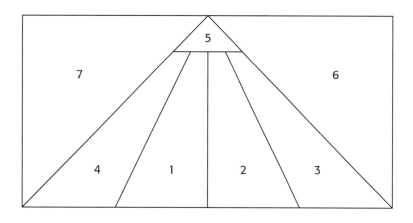

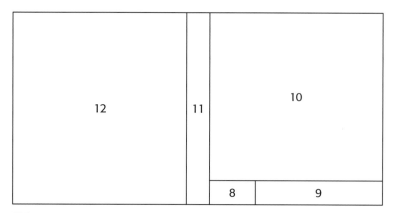

71

Block 71 Cutting List

Location	Size to Cut
6, 7	3¼" x 3¼" ◱
10, 12	2¾" x 2¾"
1, 2, 3, 4	1¾" x 3"
5, 8, 9, 11	1" x 2¾"

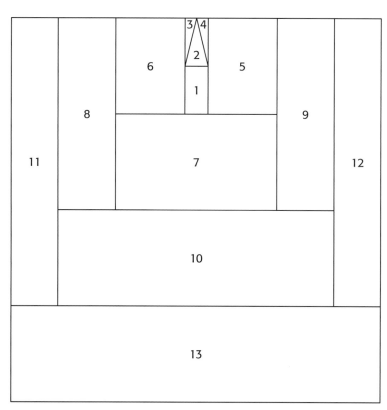

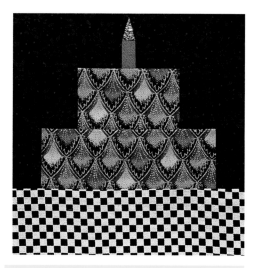

72

Block 72 Cutting List

Location	Size to Cut
10, 13	1¾" x 4¾"
7	1¾" x 2½"
5, 6, 8, 9	1½" x 2¾"
11, 12	1¼" x 3¾"
1, 2, 3, 4	1" x 1"

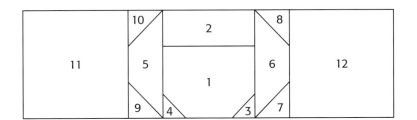

Block 73 Cutting List

Location	Size to Cut
19	2" x 3½"
1, 11, 12	1¾" x 1¾"
3, 4, 7, 8, 9, 10	1¾" x 1¾" ◹
20, 21	1½" x 2¾"
18, 22, 23, 24, 25, 26	1¼" x 3¾"
13, 16, 17	1¼" x 1½"
2, 5, 6, 14, 15	1" x 1¾"

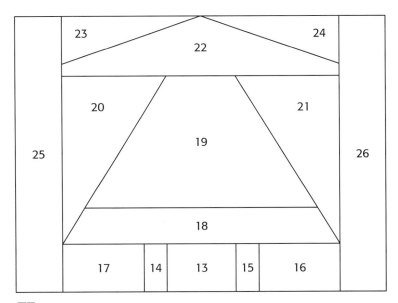

73

Block 74 Cutting List

Location	Size to Cut
1, 2, 3a, 3b	3½" x 3½" ⊠
4	2¾" x 2¾"
9, 10, 11, 12	2¼" x 2¼" ◹
7, 8	1¾" x 4¾"
5, 6	1¾" x 1¾" ◹

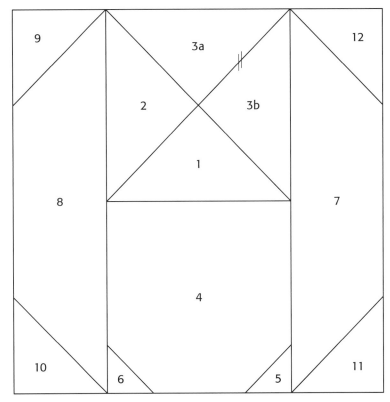

74

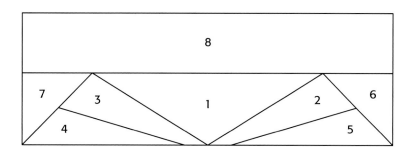

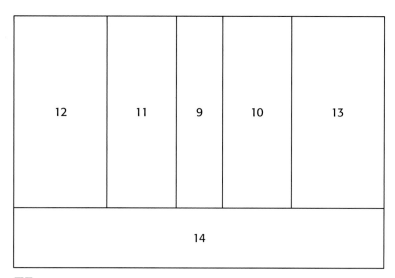

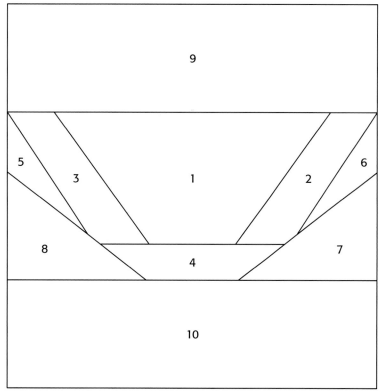

75

Block 75 Cutting List

Location	Size to Cut
6, 7	2" x 2" ◺
12, 13	1¾" x 2¾"
1, 9, 10, 11	1½" x 3¼"
8, 14	1¼" x 4¾"
2, 3, 4, 5	1¼" x 2½"

76

Block 76 Cutting List

Location	Size to Cut
1	2" x 3¾"
9, 10	1¾" x 4¾"
7, 8	1½" x 3"
2, 3, 4, 5, 6	1" x 3"

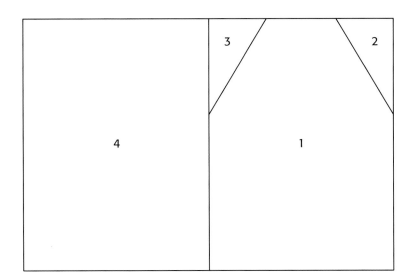

Block 77 Cutting List

Location	Size to Cut
1, 4	2¾" x 3¼"
8	2" x 5"
9	1½" x 3¼"
2, 3, 5, 6	1¼" x 2½"
7	1" x 1½"

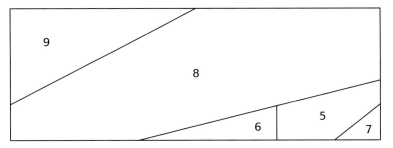

77

Block 78 Cutting List

Location	Size to Cut
12	5¼" x 5¼" ◹
8, 9	3¼" x 3¼" ◹
1	1¾" x 1¾"
11	1¾" x 1¾" ◹
10	1½" x 5¾"
2, 3, 4, 5, 14	1½" x 1½" ◹
6, 7	1¼" x 2¼"
13	1" x ½"

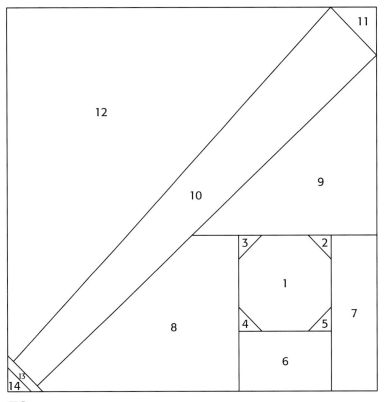

78

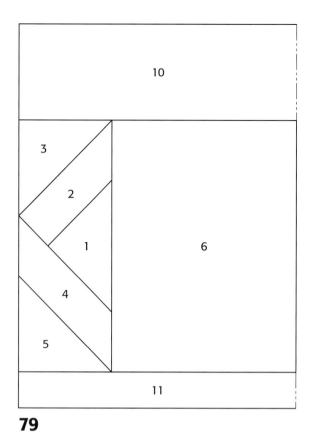
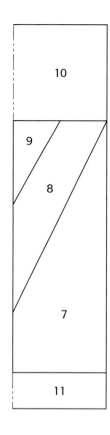

79

Block 79 Cutting List	
Location	**Size to Cut**
6	2½" x 3¼"
1, 3, 5	2¼" x 2¼" ◱
7	1¾" x 3¾"
10	1¾" x 4¾"
2, 4, 8	1¼" x 3"
11	1" x 4¾"
9	1" x 2"

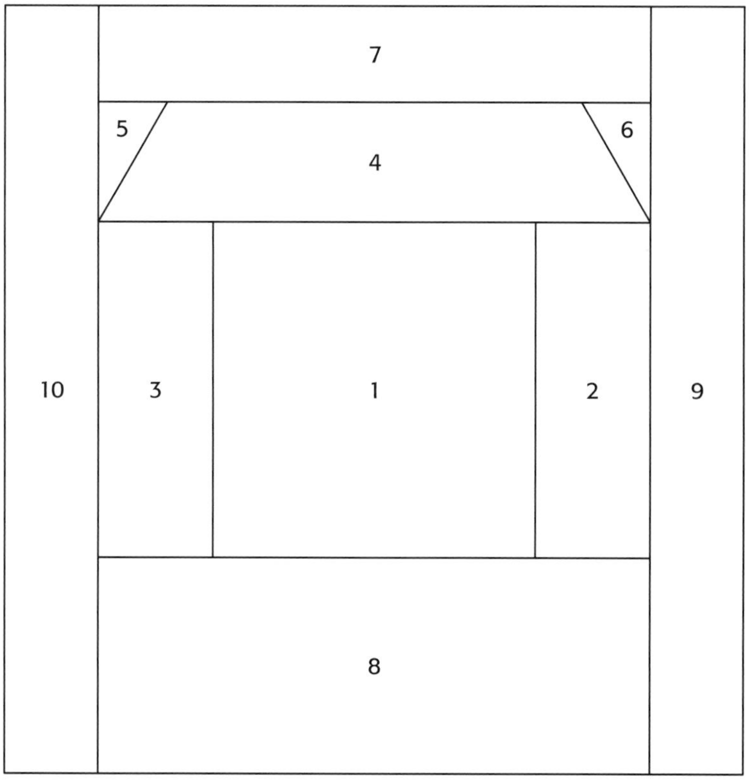

80

Block 80 Cutting List	
Location	**Size to Cut**
1	2½" x 2½"
8	1¾" x 3¾"
9, 10	1¼" x 4¾"
4, 7	1¼" x 3¾"
2, 3	1¼" x 2½"
5, 6	1" x 1½"

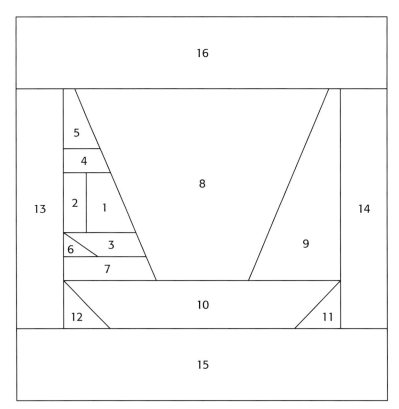

Block 81 Cutting List

Location	Size to Cut
8	3½" x 3½"
11, 12	1¾" x 1¾" ◻
15, 16	1½" x 4¾"
9	1½" x 3"
10	1¼" x 3¾"
13, 14	1¼" x 3¼"
1, 2, 3, 4, 5, 6, 7	1¼" x 1½"

81

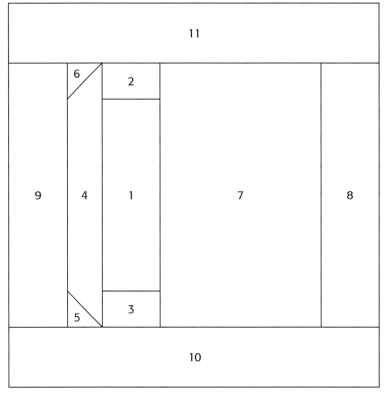

Block 82 Cutting List

Location	Size to Cut
7	2½" x 3½"
5, 6	1¾" x 1¾" ◻
10, 11	1¼" x 4¾"
1, 4, 8, 9	1¼" x 3½"
2, 3	1" x 1¼"

82

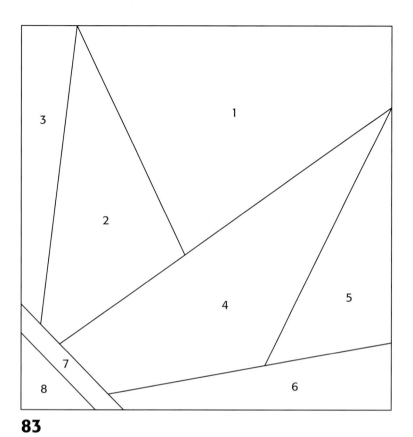

83

Block 83 Cutting List	
Location	**Size to Cut**
1	3" x 4"
4	2½" x 5½"
2	2½" x 3½"
8	2" x 2" ◻
5, 6	1¾" x 4"
3	1¼" x 4"
7	1" x 2½"

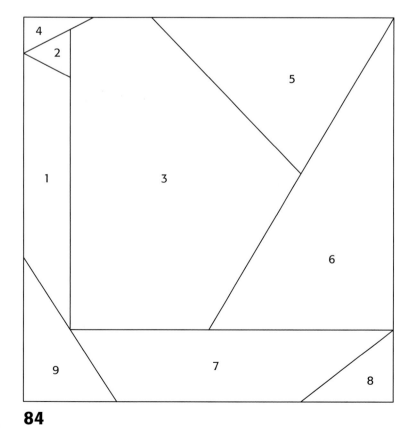

84

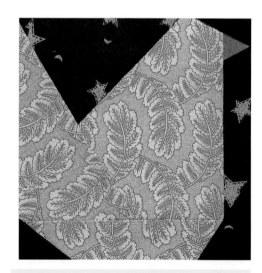

Block 84 Cutting List	
Location	**Size to Cut**
3	3¼" x 4"
6	2½" x 4½"
5	2½" x 3¼"
7	1½" x 4¼"
8, 9	1½" x 3"
1	1¼" x 3½"
2	1½" x 1½"
4	1" x 1½"

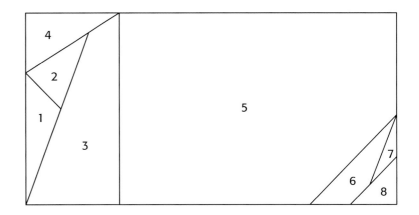

Block 85 Cutting List

Location	Size to Cut
12	2¾" x 5"
5	2¾" x 3¾"
13	2¾" x 2¾" ◪
3	1¾" x 3"
2, 4	1½" x 2"
14	1¼" x 3"
1, 6, 7, 8, 9, 10, 11	1" x 2½"

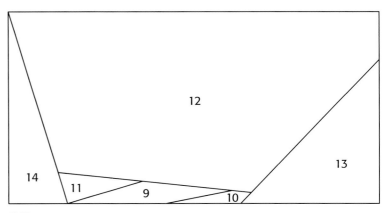

85

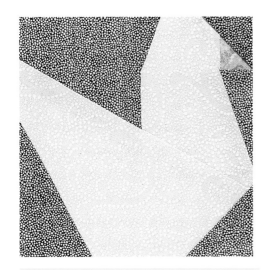

Block 86 Cutting List

Location	Size to Cut
8	2¾" x 5¼"
7	2¾" x 2¾"
4, 10	2½" x 2½" ◪
5	2¼" x 4½"
9	1¾" x 3¾"
1	1¾" x 1¾" ◪
3	1¼" x 2½"
2, 6	1" x 2"

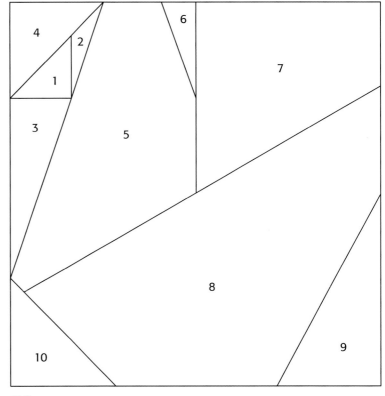

86

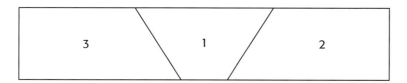

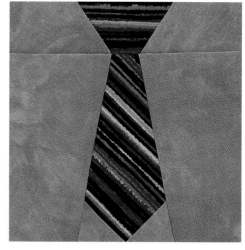

87

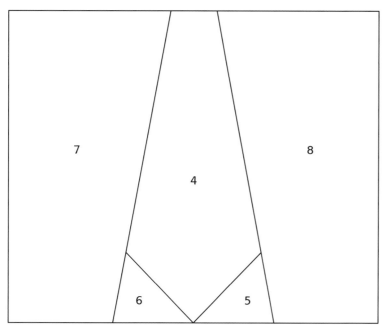

Block 87 Cutting List

Location	Size to Cut
7, 8	2½" x 4¼"
2, 3	2" x 2½"
4	2¼" x 4"
1, 5, 6	1½" x 2¼"

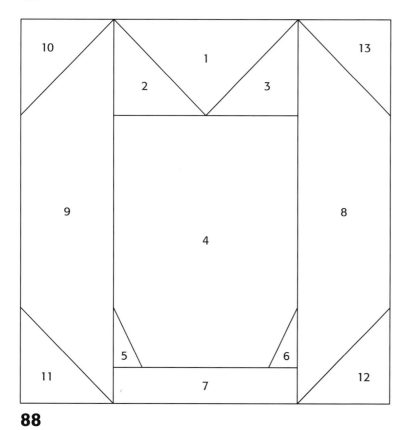

88

Block 88 Cutting List

Location	Size to Cut
4	2¾" x 3¼"
2, 3, 10, 11, 12, 13	2¼" x 2¼" ◻
8, 9	1¾" x 4¾"
1	1¾" x 2¾"
7	1" x 2¾"
5, 6	1" x 1½"

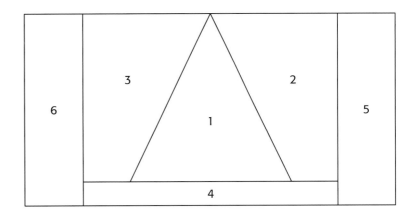

Block 89 Cutting List

Location	Size to Cut
1	2½" x 2½"
8, 9	2" x 2" ◨
2, 3	2" x 2¾"
7	2" x 2¼"
5, 6, 11, 12, 13, 14	1½" x 3"
10	1¼ x 2¼"
4	1" x 3½"

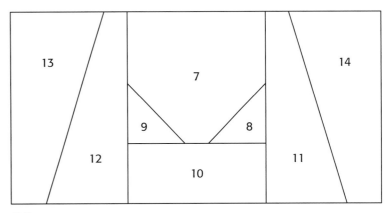

89

Block 90 Cutting List

Location	Size to Cut
8, 9	2¾" x 2¾" ◨
2, 3, 6, 7	2¼" x 2¼" ◨
14	1¾" x 4¾"
11, 12, 15, 16	1¾" x 1¾" ◨
10	1½" x 4¾"
4, 5	1¼" x 4½"
1, 13c, 13b	1¼" x 2½"
13a	1¼" x 1"

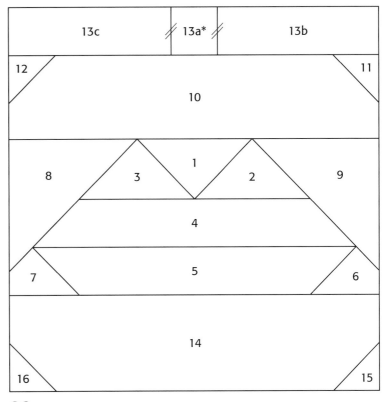

90

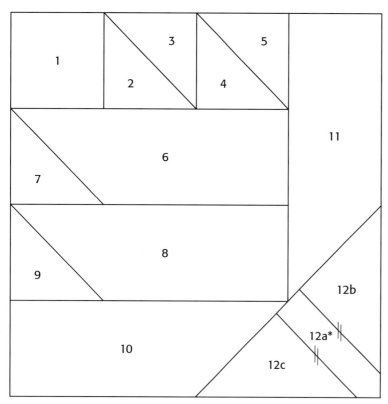

91

Block 91 Cutting List

Location	Size to Cut
12b, 12c	3¼" x 3¼" ⊠
2, 3, 4, 5, 7, 9	2¼" x 2¼" ◺
6, 8, 10, 11	1¾" x 3¾"
1	1¾" x 1¾"
12a	1" x 2"

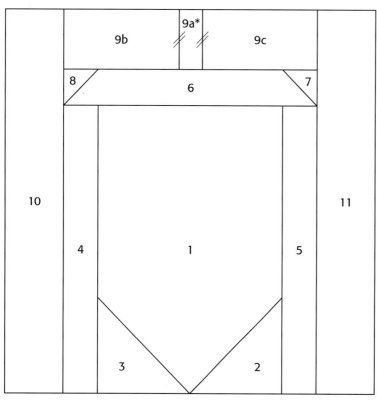

92

Block 92 Cutting List

Location	Size to Cut
1	2¾" x 3¾"
2, 3	2¼" x 2¼" ◺
7, 8	1¾" x 1¾" ◺
10, 11	1¼" x 4¾"
9b, 9c	1¼" x 2"
4, 5, 6	1" x 3¾"
9a	1" x 1¼"

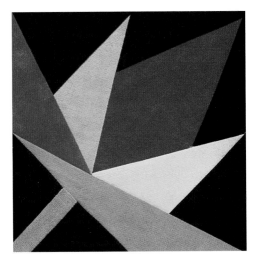

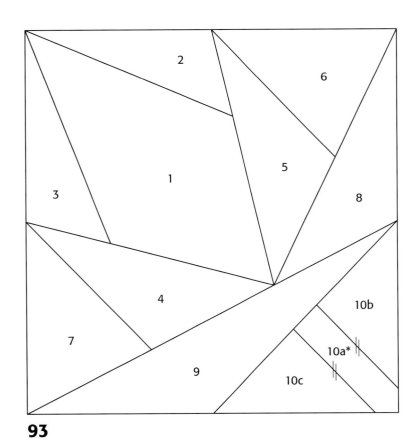

Block 93 Cutting List

Location	Size to Cut
10b, 10c	2½" x 2½" ◺
1	2½" x 4½"
6, 7	2" x 2½"
4, 5	1¾" x 3½"
9	1½" x 5½"
2, 3, 8	1½" x 3¾"
10a	1" x 2¼"

93

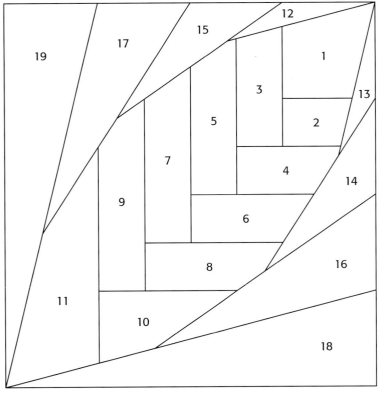

Block 94 Cutting List

Location	Size to Cut
18, 19	1¾" x 5"
11	1¾" x 3¼"
1	1¾" x 1¾"
16, 17	1½" x 4"
7, 9, 14, 15	1¼" x 3"
2, 3, 4, 5, 6, 8, 10	1¼" x 2¼"
12, 13	1" x 2½"

94

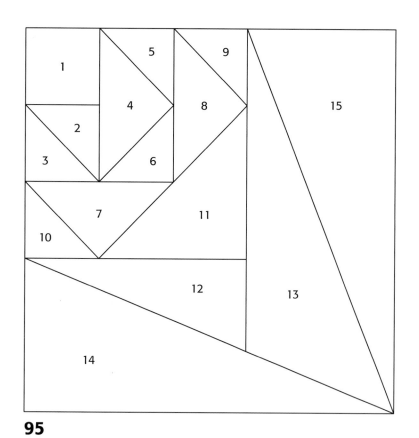

95

Block 95 Cutting List	
Location	**Size to Cut**
4, 7, 8	3¼" x 3¼" ⊠
11	3" x 3" ◺
13, 14, 15	2¼" x 5¼"
2, 3, 5, 6, 9, 10	2¼" x 2¼" ◺
12	1½" x 3"
1	1½" x 1½"

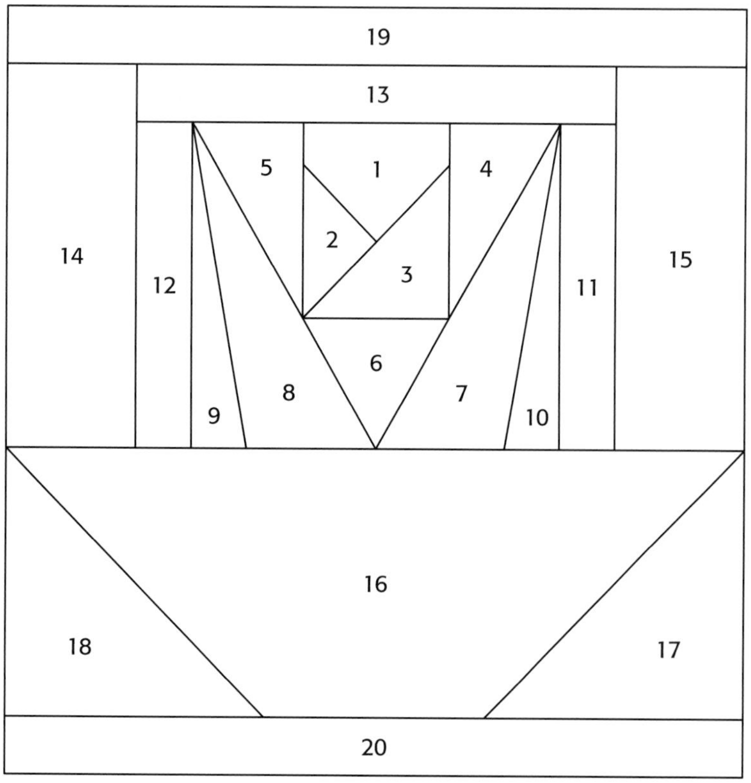

96

Block 96 Cutting List	
Location	**Size to Cut**
17, 18	2¾" x 2¾" ◺
16	2" x 4¾"
2, 3	2" x 2" ◺
14, 15	1½" x 2¾"
1, 4, 5, 6	1½" x 1½"
7, 8	1¼" x 3"
19, 20	1" x 4¾"
9, 10, 11, 12, 13	1" x 3¼"

Block 97 Cutting List

Location	Size to Cut
4, 5	2¼" x 2¼"
14, 15	1¼" x 4¾"
1	1¼" x 2¼"
6, 7, 8, 9, 12, 13	1" x 4"
10, 11	1" x 2"
2, 3	1" x 1"

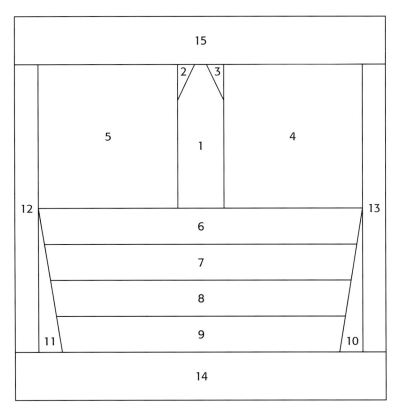

97

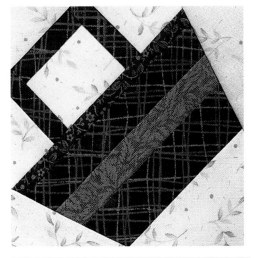

Block 98 Cutting List

Location	Size to Cut
12	3¼" x 3¼" ◺
5, 6, 7	2¼" x 2¼" ◺
1	1¾" x 2"
11	1½" x 4½"
13, 14	1½" x 3½"
9, 10	1¼" x 5"
8	1" x 5"
2, 3, 4	1" x 2¼"

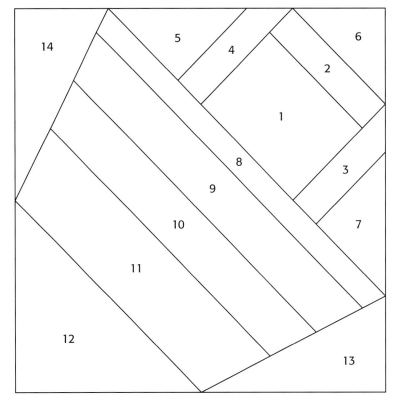

98

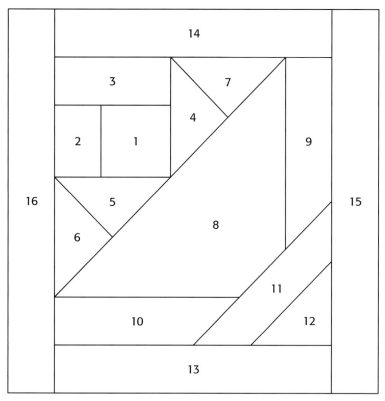

99

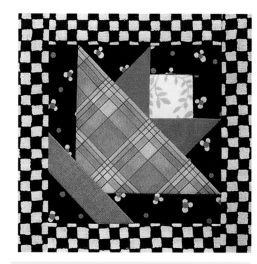

Block 99 Cutting List

Location	Size to Cut
4, 5, 6, 7	2¾" x 2¾" ⊠
12	2¼" x 2¼" ◺
8	2" x 4¼"
1	1½" x 1½"
13, 14, 15, 16	1¼" x 4¾"
2, 3, 9, 10, 11	1¼" x 2¾"

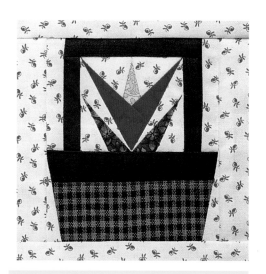

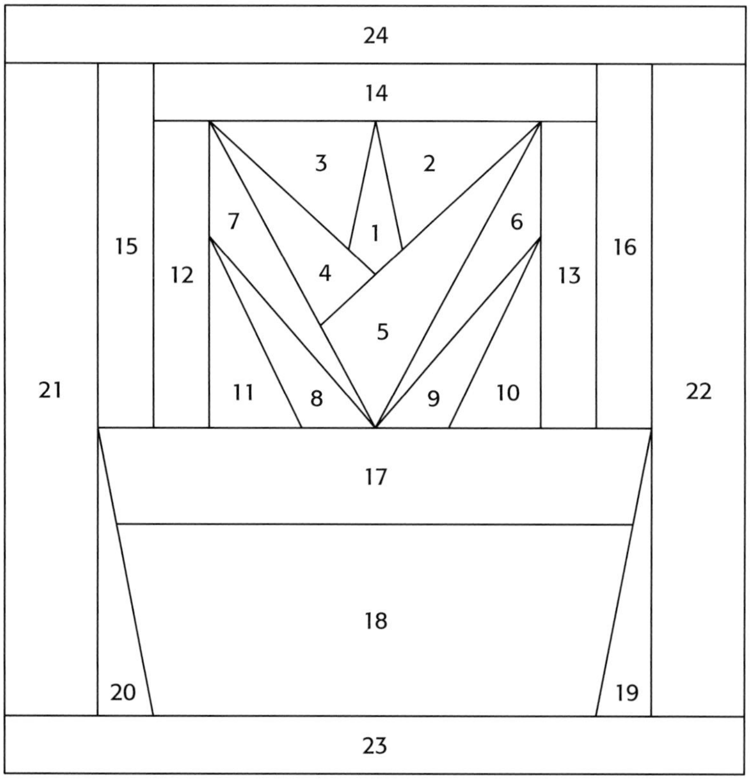

100

Block 100 Cutting List

Location	Size to Cut
18	1¾" x 3¾"
17, 21, 22	1¼" x 4"
5	1¼" x 2½"
2, 3	1¼" x 1½"
23, 24	1" x 4¾"
14, 15, 16, 19, 20	1" x 3"
1, 4, 6, 7, 8, 9, 10, 11, 12, 13	1" x 2½"

Block 101 Cutting List

Location	Size to Cut
12, 13, 14	3" x 3" ◹
9, 10	2¾" x 2¾" ◺
7	2¼" x 2¼" ◹
8	2" x 4"
1	2" x 2¼"
5, 6	1¼" x 2½"
11	1" x 4"
2, 3, 4	1" x 2¾"

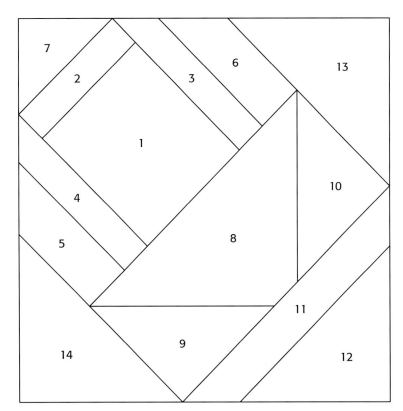

101

Block 102 Cutting List

Location	Size to Cut
18	2¼" x 2¼" ◹
16, 17	2" x 4½"
3, 15	2" x 3"
8, 9	2" x 2" ◹
1, 2	1½" x 1½"
4, 5, 6, 7, 10, 11, 14	1¼" x 3½"
12, 13	1" x 2"

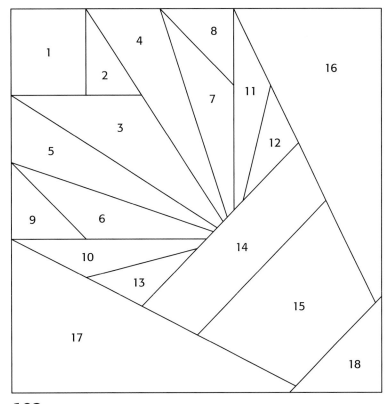

102

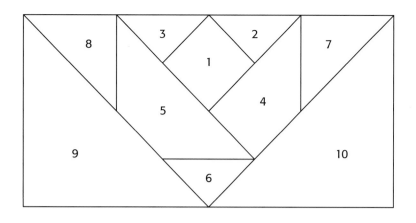

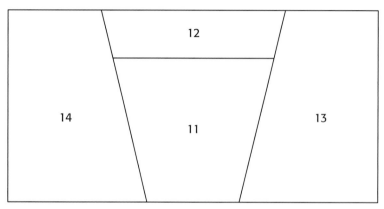

103

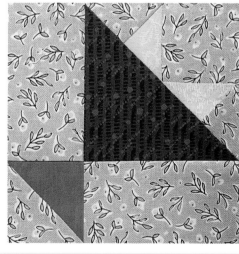

Block 103 Cutting List

Location	Size to Cut
9, 10	3¼" x 3¼" ◺
2, 3, 6	2½" x 2½" ⊠
11	2¼" x 2½"
7, 8	2¼" x 2¼" ◺
13, 14	2" x 3"
4, 5, 12	1½" x 2¾"
1	1½" x 1½"

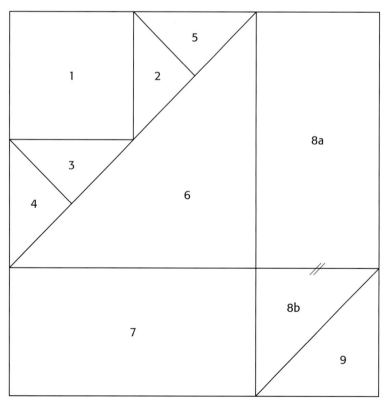

104

Block 104 Cutting List

Location	Size to Cut
6	4¼" x 4¼" ◺
8b, 9	2¾" x 2¾" ◺
2, 3, 4, 5	2¾" x 2¾" ⊠
7, 8a	2" x 3½"
1	2" x 2"

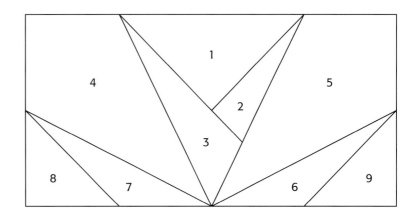

Block 105 Cutting List

Location	Size to Cut
1	2¾" x 2¾" ◨
4, 5, 10	2¼" x 3½"
8, 9	2¼" x 2¼" ◨
14, 15	1¾" x 1¾" ◨
3, 11, 12, 16, 17	1½" x 3"
2, 6, 7, 13	1" x 3½"

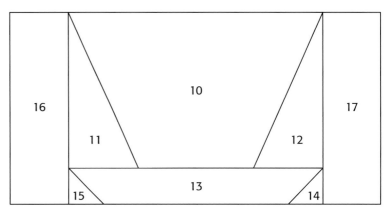

105

Block 106 Cutting List

Location	Size to Cut
20	3¼" x 3¼" ◨
4, 10, 11, 15	2¼" x 2¼" ◨
19	2" x 4½"
16, 17	1¾" x 2½"
2, 3, 9	1¾" x 1¾" ◨
21, 22	1½" x 3½"
1, 5, 6, 7, 8	1¼" x 2"
12, 13, 14, 18	1" x 4½"

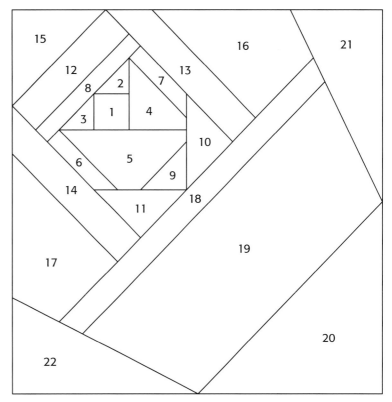

106

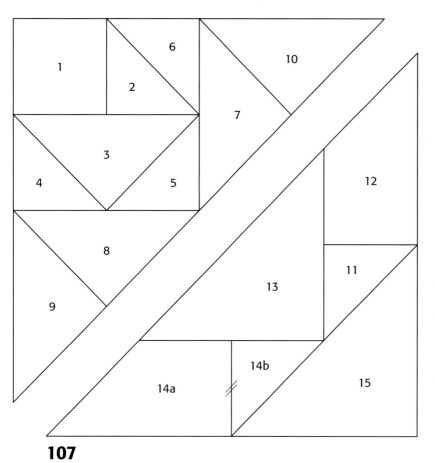

107

Block 107 Cutting List	
Location	**Size to Cut**
3, 7, 8, 9, 10	3½" x 3½" ⊠
13, 15	3¼" x 3¼" ◺
2, 4, 5, 6, 11, 14b	2¼" x 2¼" ◹
12, 14a	1¾" x 2¾"
1	1¾" x 1¾"

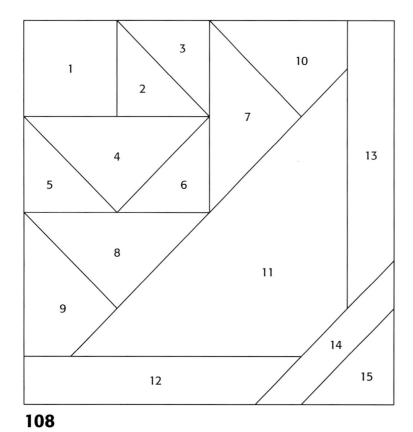

108

Block 108 Cutting List	
Location	**Size to Cut**
4, 7, 8, 9, 10	3½" x 3½" ⊠
11	2½" x 5"
2, 3, 5, 6, 15	2¼" x 2¼" ◺
1	1¾" x 1¾"
12, 13	1¼" x 3¾"
14	1" x 3½"

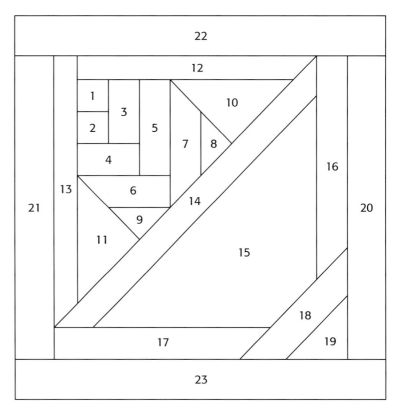

109

Block 109 Cutting List

Location	Size to Cut
10, 11	2¾" x 2¾" ⊠
15	2" x 4½"
19	2" x 2" ◺
14, 20, 21, 22, 23	1" x 4¾"
12, 13, 16, 17, 18	1" x 3½"
5, 6, 7, 8, 9	1" x 2"
1, 2, 3, 4	1" x 1¼"

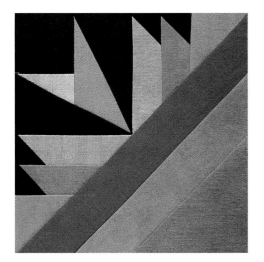

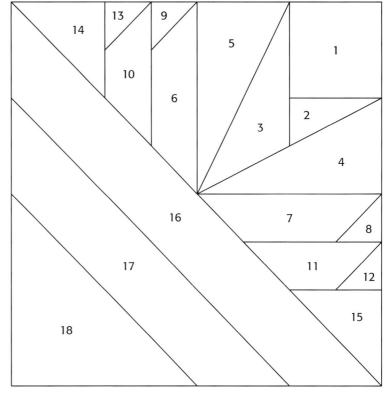

110

Block 110 Cutting List

Location	Size to Cut
18	3¼" x 3¼" ◺
14, 15	2¼" x 2¼" ◺
1	1¾" x 1¾"
8, 9, 12, 13	1¾" x 1¾" ◺
16, 17	1½" x 6½"
3, 4, 5, 6, 7	1½" x 3"
2, 10, 11	1¼" x 2½"

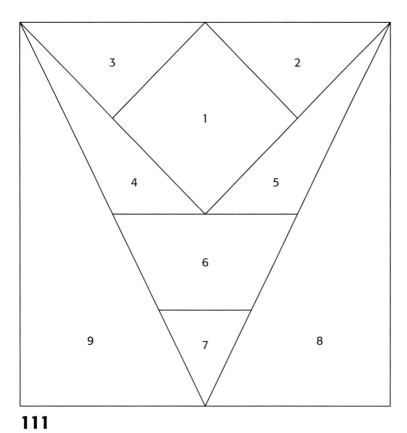

111

Block 111 Cutting List

Location	Size to Cut
2, 3	2¾" x 2¾" ◹
8, 9	2½" x 5½"
1	2½" x 2½"
7	2" x 2"
6	1½" x 2¾"
4, 5	1¼" x 3½"

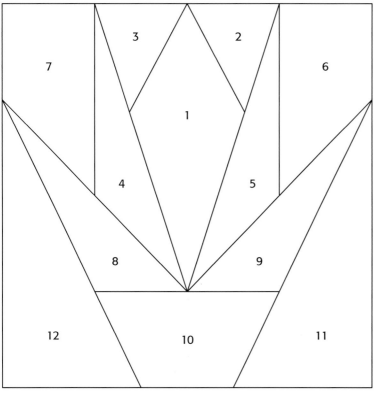

112

Block 112 Cutting List

Location	Size to Cut
11, 12	2" x 4½"
1	2" x 3¾"
6, 7, 10	1¾" x 2¾"
2, 3	1½" x 2"
4, 5, 8, 9	1¼" x 4"

Block 113 Cutting List

Location	Size to Cut
18, 19	2½" x 3"
20, 21	2¼" x 4¾"
16	1¾" x 3"
17	1¾" x 2"
1, 2, 3, 4, 5, 6, 7, 8, 9, 10, 11, 12, 13, 14, 15	1" x 2"

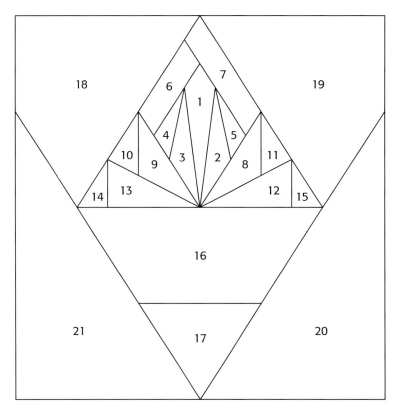

113

Block 114 Cutting List

Location	Size to Cut
5, 6, 7	2" x 3"
10, 11, 14, 15	1½" x 3"
8, 9, 12, 13	1¼" x 5"
1, 2, 3, 4	1¼" x 1¾"

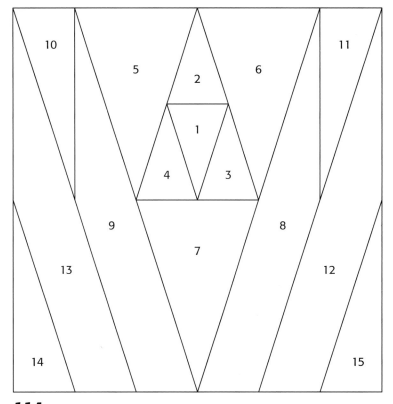

114

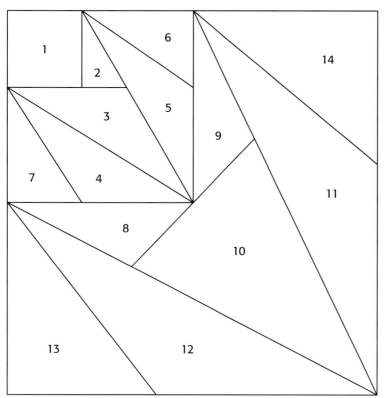

115

Block 115 Cutting List	
Location	**Size to Cut**
10	2½" x 3½"
13, 14	2" x 3½"
3	2" x 2¾"
11, 12	1¾" x 5½"
1, 2	1½" x 1½"
4, 5, 6, 7, 8, 9	1¼" x 3"

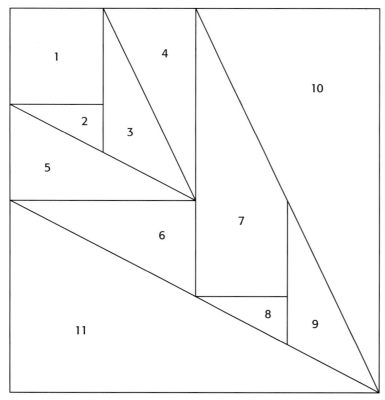

116

Block 116 Cutting List	
Location	**Size to Cut**
10, 11	2½" x 5½"
3, 9	1¾" x 2¾"
1	1¾" x 1¾"
4, 5, 6	1¾" x 3"
7	1½" x 3¾"
2, 8	1¼" x 1¾"

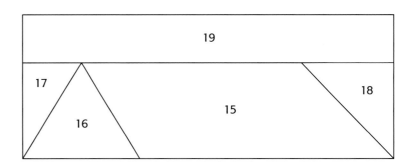

Block 117 Cutting List

Location	Size to Cut
1, 4, 5, 18	2¼" x 2¼" ◺
2, 16	2" x 2"
15	1¾" x 4"
3	1¾" x 2½"
6, 7	1¾" x 1¾" ◺
19	1¼" x 4¾"
13a, 13b, 17	1¼" x 2¼"
8, 9, 10, 11, 12, 14	1" x 3½"

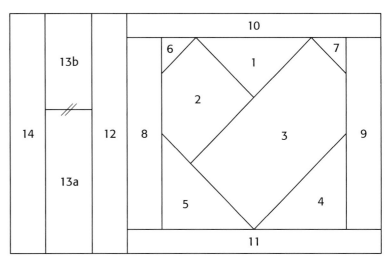

117

Block 118 Cutting List

Location	Size to Cut
3	3¼" x 4¾"
2	2¼" x 3¼"
1	2¼" x 2¼"
4, 5	2¼" x 2¼" ◺

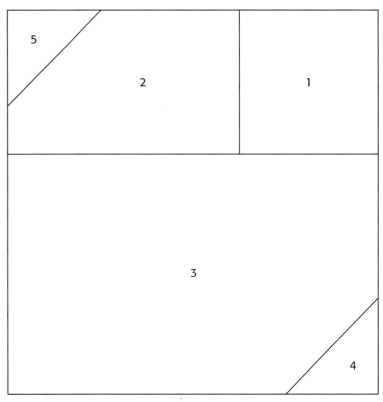

118

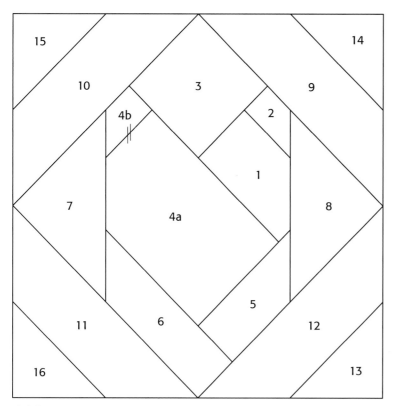

119

Block 119 Cutting List

Location	Size to Cut
7, 8	3½" x 3½" ⊠
4a	2" x 2¾"
13, 14, 15, 16	2¼" x 2¼" ◺
3	1¾" x 1¾"
9, 10, 11, 12	1½" x 3½"
1	1½" x 2"
5, 6	1¼" x 2¾"
2, 4b	1" x 1½"

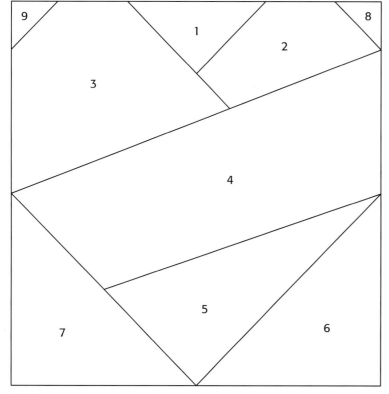

120

Block 120 Cutting List

Location	Size to Cut
6, 7	3¼" x 3¼" ◺
3	3" x 3"
1	2¾" x 2¾" ⊠
4	2" x 5½"
5	2" x 4"
2	2" x 2¼"
8, 9	1¾" x 1¾" ◺

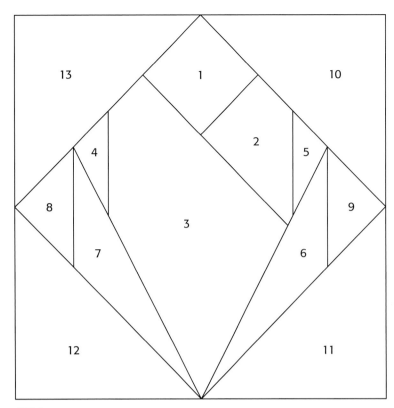

Block 121 Cutting List

Location	Size to Cut
10, 11, 12, 13	3¼" x 3¼" ◺
3	2¾" x 3½"
8, 9	2¼" x 2¼" ◺
2	1½" x 2"
1	1½" x 1½"
6, 7	1¼" x 3½"
4, 5	1" x 2"

121

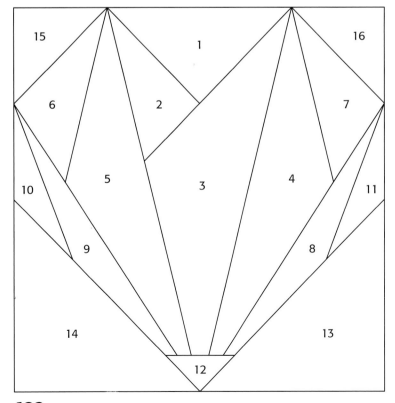

Block 122 Cutting List

Location	Size to Cut
1	3½" x 3½" ⊠
13, 14	3¼" x 3¼" ◺
3	2½" x 4"
15, 16	2¼" x 2¼" ◺
4, 5	1½" x 4½"
2, 6, 7	1½" x 3"
8, 9, 10, 11	1" x 4"
12	1" x 1½"

122

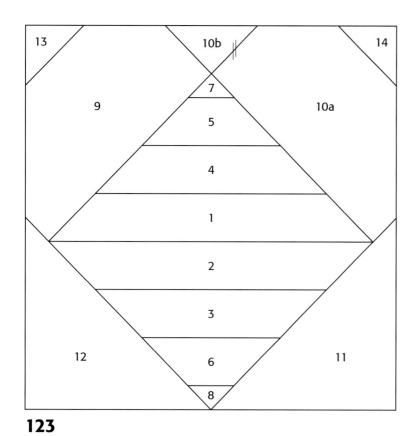

123

Block 123 Cutting List	
Location	**Size to Cut**
11, 12	3¼" x 3¼" ◺
10b	2½" x 2½" ⊠
9, 10a	2" x 3¼"
7, 8, 13, 14	1¾" x 1¾" ◺
1, 2	1" x 4"
3, 4, 5, 6	1" x 3½"

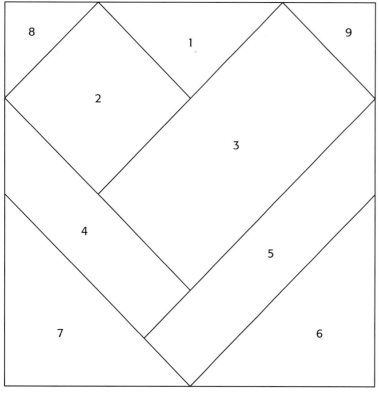

124

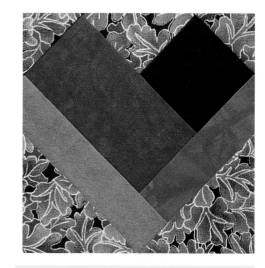

Block 124 Cutting List	
Location	**Size to Cut**
1	3½" x 3½" ⊠
6, 7	3¼" x 3¼" ◺
8, 9	2¼" x 2¼" ◺
3	2" x 3½"
2	2" x 2"
4, 5	1½" x 4½"

Block 125 Cutting List

Location	Size to Cut
12, 16, 17	3¼" x 3¼" ◻
1	2¼" x 3"
6, 7, 10, 11, 15b	2½" x 2½" ⊠
14, 15a	2" x 3¼"
13, 18, 19	1¾" x 1¾" ◻
2, 3	1¼" x 1¾"
4, 5, 8, 9	1" x 3"

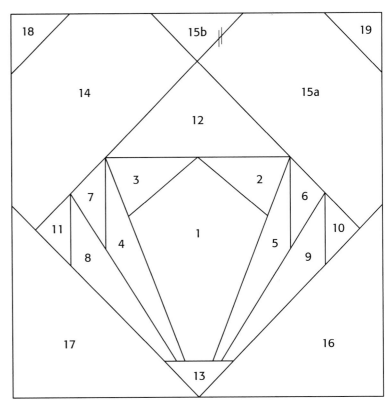

125

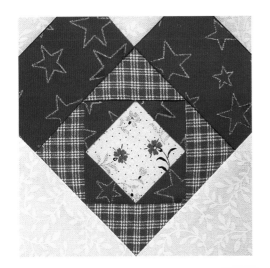

Block 126 Cutting List

Location	Size to Cut
6, 7, 8, 9	3¼" x 3¼" ⊠
12, 13	3¼" x 3¼" ◻
11b	2½" x 2½" ⊠
2, 3, 4, 5	2¼" x 2¼" ◻
10, 11a	2" x 3¼"
1	2" x 2"
14, 15	1¾" x 1¾" ◻

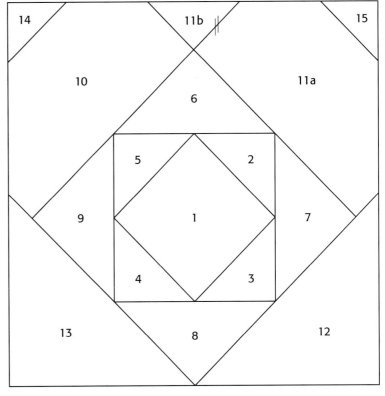

126

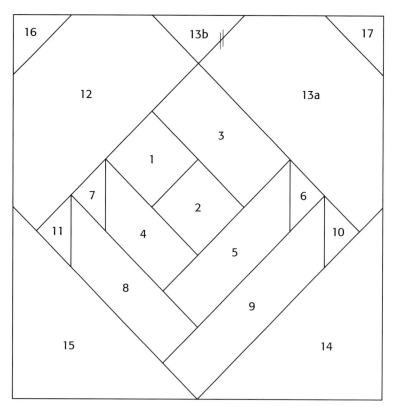

127

Block 127 Cutting List	
Location	**Size to Cut**
14, 15	3¼" x 3¼" ◺
13b	2½" x 2½" ⊠
12, 13a	2" x 3¼"
6, 7, 10, 11, 16, 17	1¾" x 1¾" ◺
8, 9	1¼" x 3¼"
3, 4, 5	1¼" x 2½"
1, 2	1¼" x 1¼"

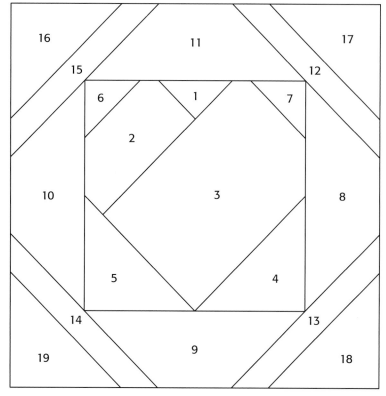

128

Block 128 Cutting List	
Location	**Size to Cut**
4, 5, 16, 17, 18, 19	2½" x 2½" ◺
1	2¼" x 2¼" ⊠
3	2" x 2¾"
6, 7	2" x 2" ◺
8, 9, 10, 11	1½" x 3"
2	1¼" x 2"
12, 13, 14, 15	1" x 3"

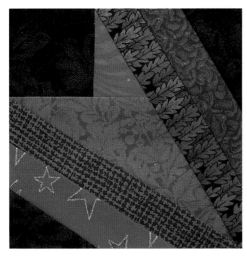

Block 129 Cutting List

Location	Size to Cut
3	3¼" x 4¾"
1	2¼" x 2¼"
2	1½" x 2¼"
4, 5	1¼" x 5½"
6, 7	1¼" x 4½"
8, 9	1½" x 3"

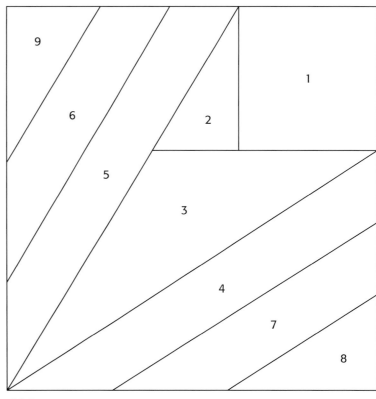

129

Block 130 Cutting List

Location	Size to Cut
12, 13	4½" x 4½" ◺
8, 9	2¼" x 2¼" ◺
1	2" x 2" ◺
3	1½" x 2½"
2	1½" x 1½"
4, 5	1½" x 1½" ◺
10, 11	1" x 4½"
6, 7	1" x 2¼"

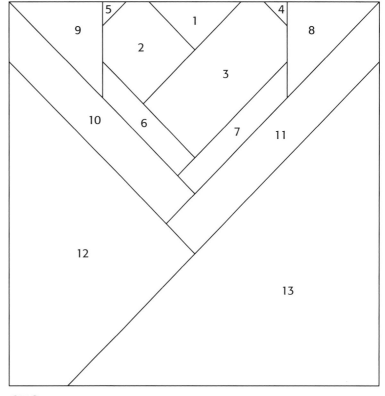

130

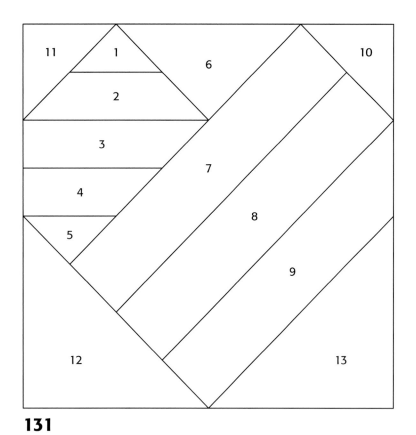

131

Block 131 Cutting List

Location	Size to Cut
6	3½" x 3½" ⊠
12, 13	3¼" x 3¼" ◨
10, 11	2¼" x 2¼" ◨
7, 8, 9	1¼" x 4¼"
3	1" x 2¾"
2, 4	1" x 2½"
1, 5	1" x 2"

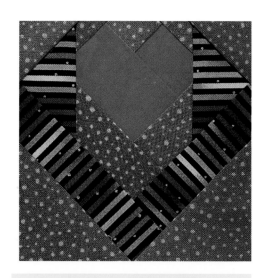

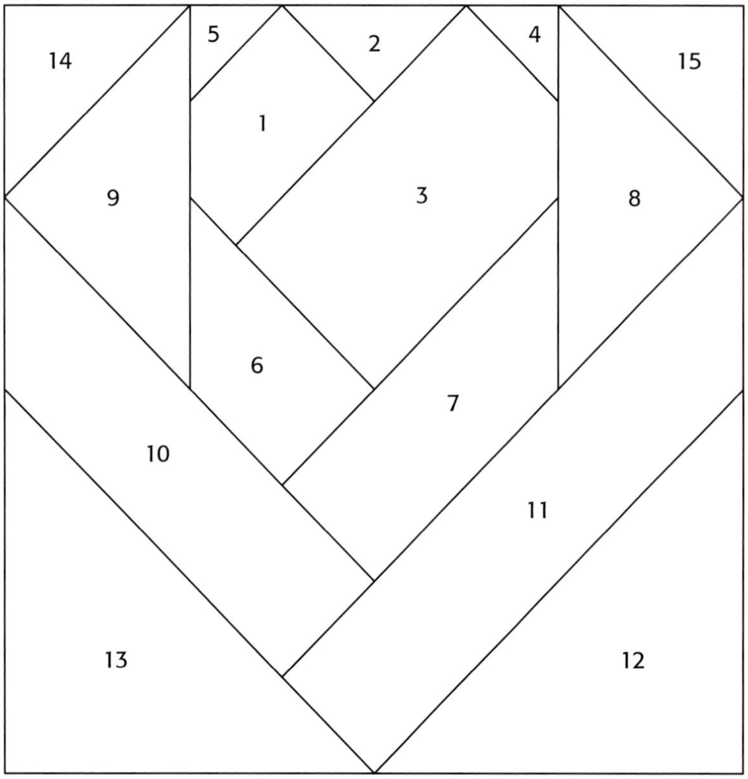

132

Block 132 Cutting List

Location	Size to Cut
8, 9	3½" x 3½" ⊠
12, 13	3¼" x 3¼" ◨
2	2½" x 2½" ⊠
14, 15	2¼" x 2¼" ◨
3	1¾" x 2¼"
4, 5	1¾" x 1¾" ◨
10, 11	1½" x 4½"
1, 6, 7	1½" x 2¾"

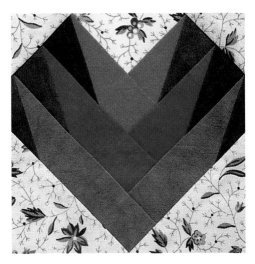

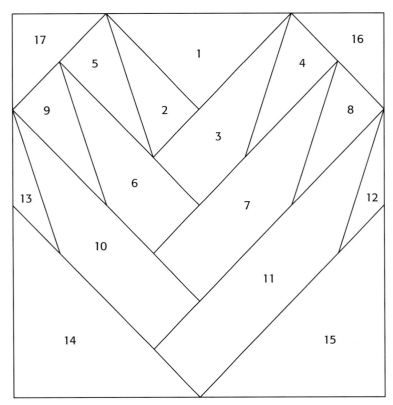

133

Block 133 Cutting List

Location	Size to Cut
1	3½" x 3½" ⊠
14, 15	3¼" x 3¼" ◹
16, 17	2¼" x 2¼" ◹
10, 11	1¼" x 4¼"
6, 7	1¼" x 3½"
3	1¼" x 2¾"
2, 4, 5, 8, 9	1¼" x 2¼"
12, 13	1" x 2¼"

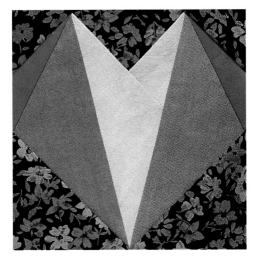

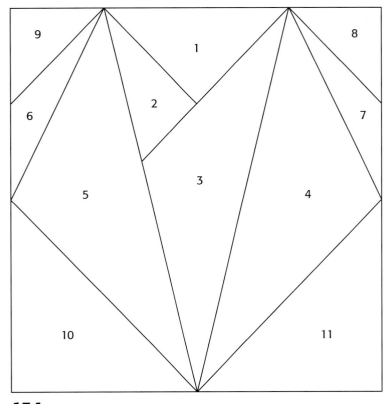

134

Block 134 Cutting List

Location	Size to Cut
1	3½" x 3½" ⊠
10, 11	3¼" x 3¼" ◹
3	2¾" x 4½"
8, 9	2¼" x 2¼" ◹
4, 5	2" x 5"
2	1½" x 2"
6, 7	1¼" x 3½"

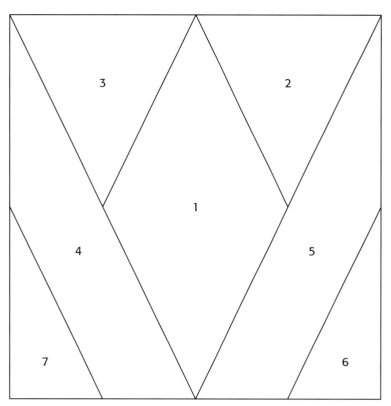

135

Block 135 Cutting List	
Location	**Size to Cut**
1	2¾" x 4¾"
2, 3	2½" x 3"
4, 5	1½" x 5½"
6, 7	1½" x 3½"

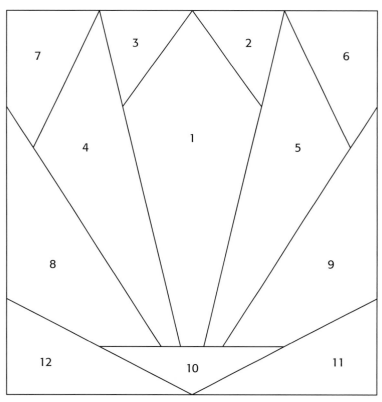

136

Block 136 Cutting List	
Location	**Size to Cut**
1	2¼" x 4¼"
8, 9	1¾" x 3¾"
4, 5	1½" x 4½"
11, 12	1½" x 3½"
2, 3, 6, 7	1½" x 2½"
10	1¼" x 3"

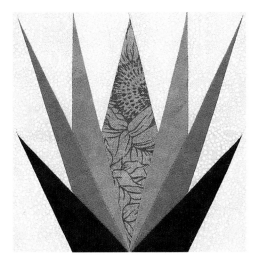

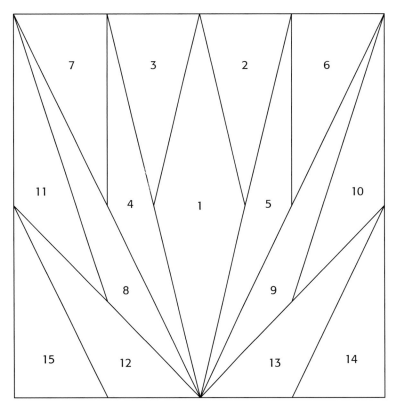

Block 137 Cutting List

Location	Size to Cut
1	1½" x 4¾"
12, 13	1½" x 3¾"
2, 3, 14, 15	1½" x 3½"
6, 7	1½" x 2¾"
10, 11	1¼" x 4"
4, 5, 8, 9	1" x 5"

137

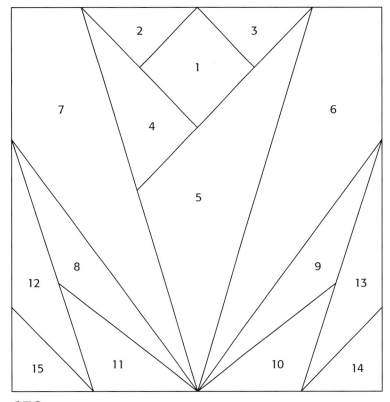

Block 138 Cutting List

Location	Size to Cut
5	2½" x 4½"
2, 3	2¼" x 2¼" ◻
14, 15	2" x 2" ◻
6, 7	1¾" x 5¼"
4	1½" x 2½"
1	1½" x 1½"
8, 9	1¼" x 4¼"
10, 11, 12, 13	1¼" x 3½"

138

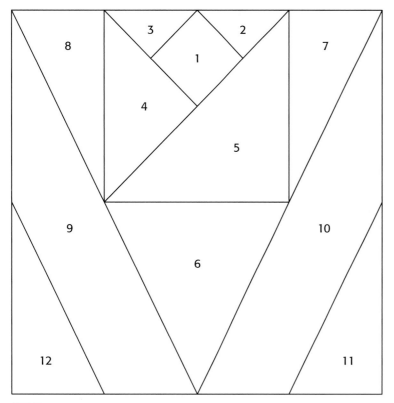

139

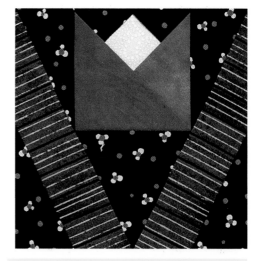

Block 139 Cutting List	
Location	Size to Cut
5	3¼" x 3¼" ◻
4	2¾" x 2¾" ◻
6	2¾" x 2¾"
2, 3	2" x 2" ◻
7, 8	1¾" x 2¾"
9, 10	1½" x 5¼"
11, 12	1½" x 3½"
1	1½" x 1½"

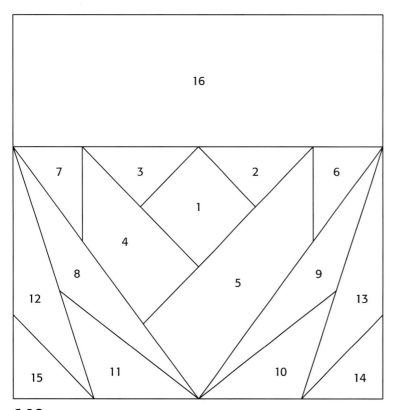

140

Block 140 Cutting List	
Location	Size to Cut
2, 3, 6, 7, 14, 15	2¼" x 2¼" ◻
16	2" x 4¾"
4, 5	1½" x 3½"
1	1½" x 1½"
12, 13	1¼" x 3½"
10, 11	1¼" x 2½"
8, 9	1" x 4¼"

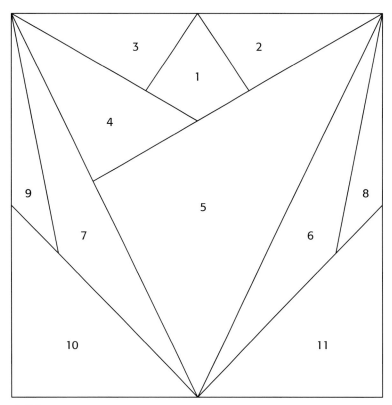

141

Block 141 Cutting List	
Location	**Size to Cut**
10, 11	3¼" x 3¼" ◨
5	3" x 4½"
4	2" x 3"
2, 3	2" x 2½"
1	2" x 2"
6, 7	1½" x 5¼"
8, 9	1" x 3½"

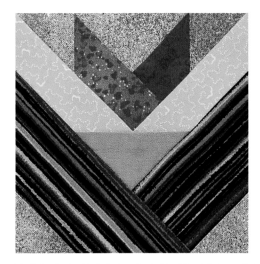

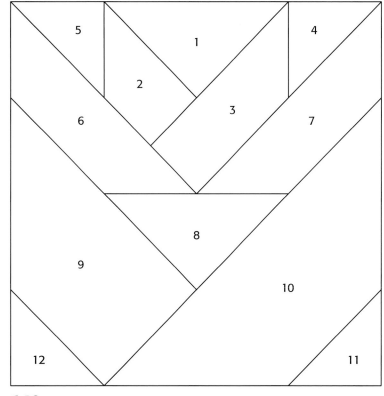

142

Block 142 Cutting List	
Location	**Size to Cut**
1, 8	3½" x 3½" ⊠
4, 5, 11, 12	2¼" x 2¼" ◨
10	2" x 5½"
9	2" x 3¾"
6, 7	1¼" x 3½"
2, 3	1¼" x 3"

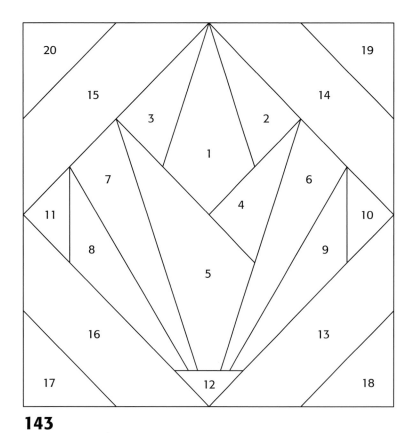

143

Block 143 Cutting List	
Location	**Size to Cut**
17, 18, 19, 20	2¼" x 2¼" ◺
5	2" x 3¼"
10, 11, 12	2" x 2" ◹
1	1½" x 2½"
6, 7, 13, 14, 15, 16	1¼" x 3½"
2, 3, 4	1¼" x 2¼"
8, 9	1" x 3¼"

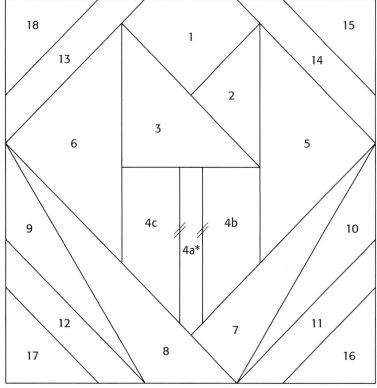

144

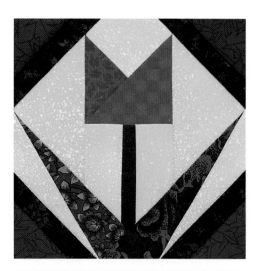

Block 144 Cutting List	
Location	**Size to Cut**
3, 5, 6	3" x 3" ◺
2	3" x 3" ⊠
15, 16, 17, 18	2¼" x 2¼" ◺
1	1¾" x 1¾"
7, 8	1½" x 4½"
4a, 4b, 4c	1¼" x 2½"
9, 10, 11, 12, 13, 14	1" x 3¾"

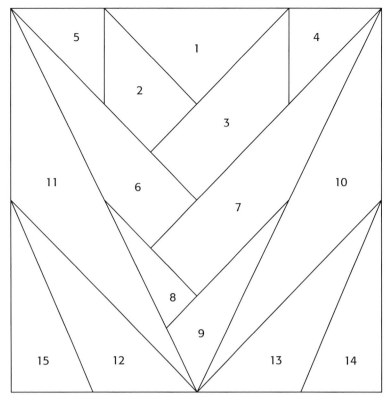

Block 145 Cutting List

Location	Size to Cut
1	2¾" x 2¾" ◺
4, 5	2¼" x 2¼" ◺
10, 11	1½" x 5½"
6, 7, 12, 13	1½" x 4¼"
2, 3, 9, 14, 15	1½" x 3"
8	1" x 2"

145

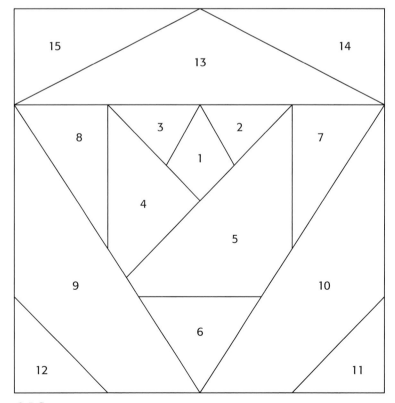

Block 146 Cutting List

Location	Size to Cut
11, 12	2¼" x 2¼" ◺
13	1¾" x 4¾"
9, 10	1¾" x 4½"
5	1¾" x 3½"
4, 6, 7, 8	1¾" x 2¼"
14, 15	1½" x 3¾"
1, 2, 3	1½" x 1½"

146

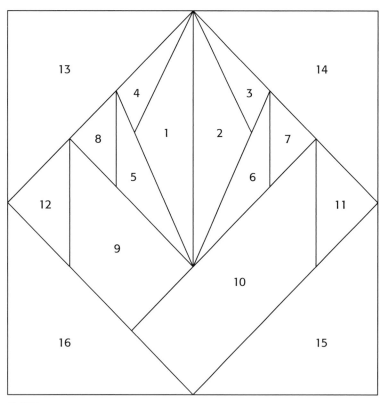

147

Block 147 Cutting List

Location	Size to Cut
13, 14, 15, 16	3¼" x 3¼" ◫
11, 12	2¼" x 2¼" ◫
7, 8	2" x 2" ◫
10	1½" x 3½"
9	1½" x 2½"
1, 2	1¼" x 3¼"
3, 4, 5, 6	1" x 2¾"

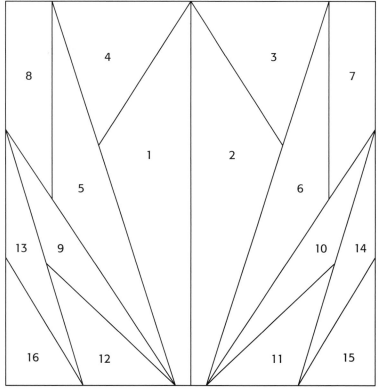

148

Block 148 Cutting List

Location	Size to Cut
3, 4	2" x 2½"
1, 2	1¾" x 4¾"
7, 8	1¾" x 2¾"
11, 12, 15, 16	1½" x 2½"
5, 6	1¼" x 5"
9, 10, 13, 14	1" x 4"

Block 149 Cutting List

Location	Size to Cut
11	3¼" x 3¼" ◺
1, 6	2" x 2"
7, 8	1¾" x 3¾"
12, 13, 14, 15	1½" x 3¾"
9, 10	1¼" x 3¼"
2, 3, 4, 5	1¼" x 2"

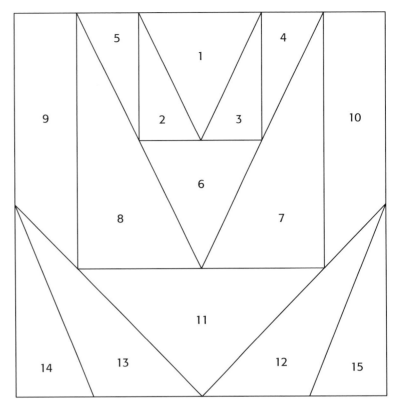

149

Block 150 Cutting List

Location	Size to Cut
4	3" x 3" ⊠
5, 11, 16, 17	3" x 3" ◺
7, 8	1¾" x 2½"
2, 3	1¾" x 1¾" ◺
6b, 6c	1¾" x 1¾"
9, 10, 14, 15	1½" x 3¾"
1	1¼" x 1¼"
6a, 12, 13	1" x 2½"

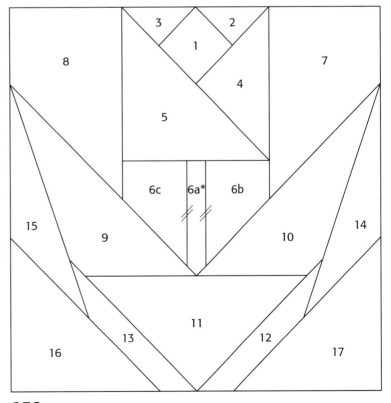

150

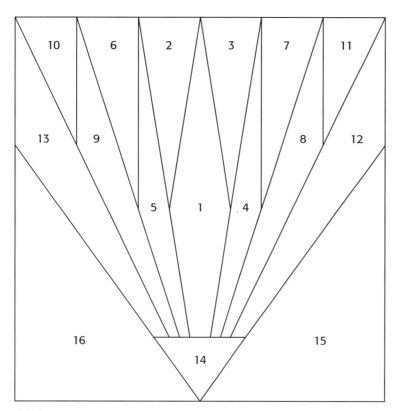

151

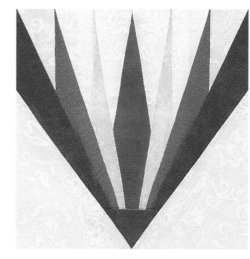

Block 151 Cutting List	
Location	**Size to Cut**
15, 16	2¼" x 4½"
14	1½" x 1½"
1, 12, 13	1¼" x 4½"
4, 5, 8, 9	1" x 4"
2, 3, 6, 7	1¼" x 3"
10, 11	1¼" x 2½"

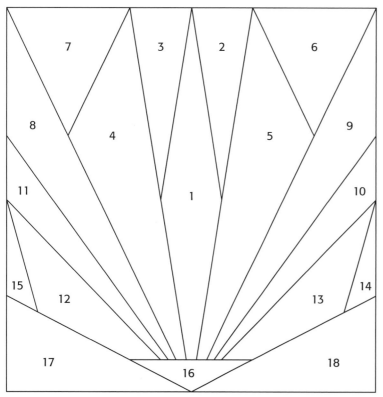

152

Block 152 Cutting List	
Location	**Size to Cut**
6, 7	2" x 2¼"
1, 4, 5	1½" x 4½"
17, 18	1½" x 3¼"
8, 9	1¼" x 4¾"
2, 3, 12, 13	1¼" x 3¼"
10, 11	1" x 3¾"
14, 15, 16	1" x 2"

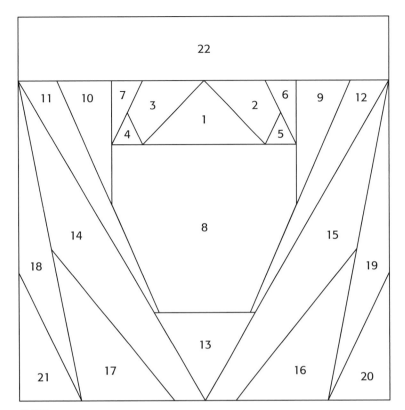

153

Block 153 Cutting List

Location	Size to Cut
8	2½" x 2½"
14, 15, 22	1½" x 4¾"
16, 17	1½" x 3"
13	1½" x 2"
1, 9, 10, 20, 21	1¼" x 2½"
2, 3, 6, 7	1¼" x 1½"
11, 12, 18, 19	1" x 4½"
4, 5	1" x 1"

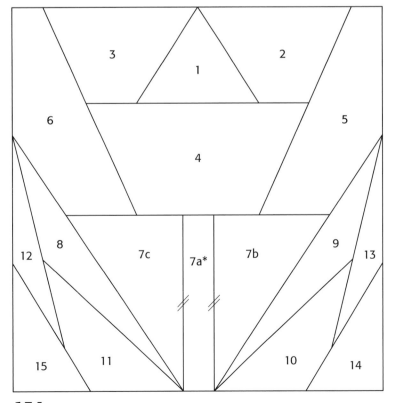

154

Block 154 Cutting List

Location	Size to Cut
2, 3	2" x 2¼"
4	1¾" x 3¼"
1, 7b, 7c	1¾" x 2½"
5, 6	1½" x 3¼"
14, 15	1½" x 2½"
10, 11	1¼" x 3"
8, 9, 12, 13	1" x 4"
7a	1" x 2½"

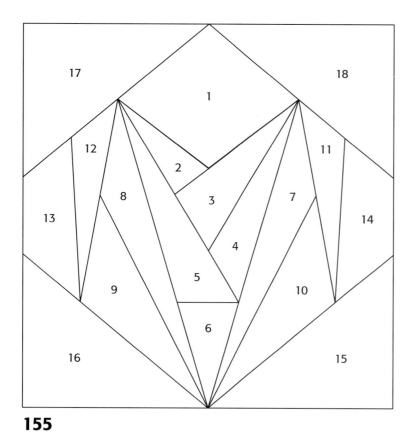

155

Block 155 Cutting List

Location	Size to Cut
15, 16, 17, 18	2" x 3½"
1	2" x 2¾"
6	1½" x 1¾"
3, 4, 5, 9, 10	1¼" x 3¼"
13, 14	1¼" x 2½"
7, 8, 11, 12	1" x 4"
2	1" x 2"

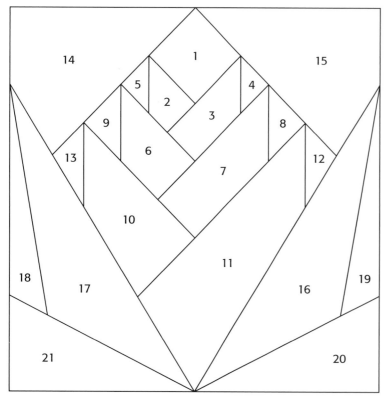

156

Block 156 Cutting List

Location	Size to Cut
14, 15	2" x 3"
4, 5, 8, 9, 12, 13	2" x 2" ◹
16, 17	1¾" x 5"
11, 20, 21	1¾" x 3½"
7, 10	1½" x 2¼"
1	1½" x 1½"
2, 3, 6	1¼" x 1¾"
18, 19	1" x 3¼"

Block 157 Cutting List

Location	Size to Cut
5	2¼" x 4¼"
2, 3, 17, 18, 19, 20	2" x 2" ◺
6, 7	1½" x 4½"
4, 11, 12	1½" x 2½"
1	1½" x 1½"
8, 9, 13, 14	1¼" x 4"
10, 15, 16	1" x 2½"

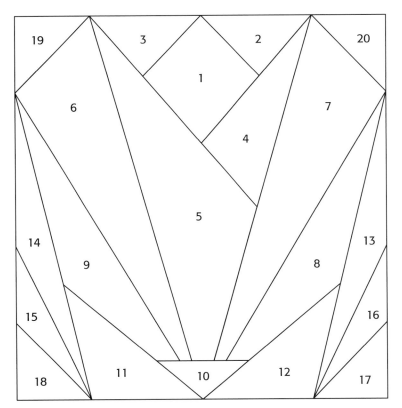

157

Block 158 Cutting List

Location	Size to Cut
5	4¼" x 4¼" ⊠
1, 4b	2¾" x 2¾" ⊠
3	2½" x 2½"
10, 11	2¼" x 2¼" ◺
4a	2" x 2½"
12, 13	2" x 2" ◺
6, 7, 8, 9	1¼" x 4¼"
2	1" x 2"

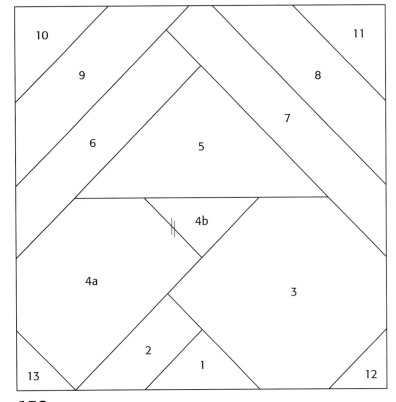

158

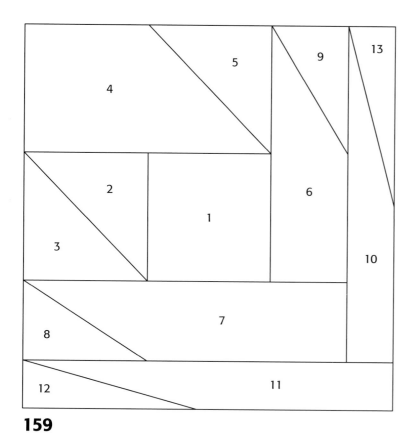

159

Block 159 Cutting List	
Location	**Size to Cut**
2, 3, 5	2¾" x 2¾" ◻
4	2" x 3½"
1	2" x 2"
6, 7	1½" x 4¼"
10, 11	1¼" x 4¾"
8, 9, 12, 13	1¼" x 3"

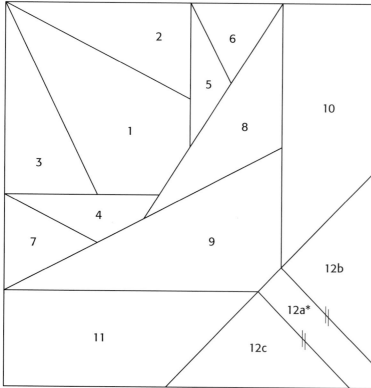

160

Block 160 Cutting List	
Location	**Size to Cut**
12b, 12c	2¾" x 2¾" ◻
1	2" x 3¼"
9	1¾" x 4"
10, 11	1¾" x 3½"
2, 3, 8	1½" x 3½"
6, 7	1½" x 2"
4, 5, 12a	1" x 2¼"

Block 161 Cutting List

Location	Size to Cut
13, 14, 15	2¼" x 2¼" ◱
16, 17	1¾" x 3¾"
1	1¾" x 1¾"
3, 4, 5	1½" x 2½"
9, 10	1½" x 1½"
18	1¼" x 6½"
7, 8, 11, 12	1¼" x 3"
2, 6	1" x 1¾"

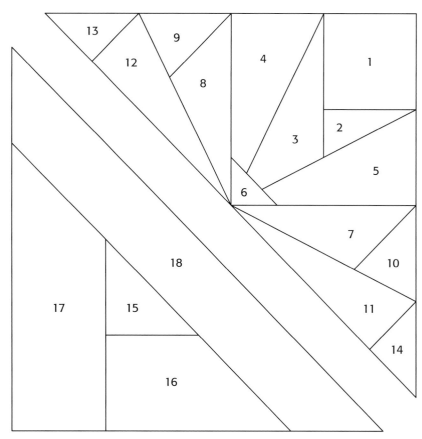

161

Block 162 Cutting List

Location	Size to Cut
6, 7	2¾" x 3¾"
15	2¾" x 2¾" ◱
5	2" x 3½"
14	1½" x 5"
1, 2, 3	1½" x 2½"
10, 11	1¼" x 3"
4	1¼" x 2"
8, 9, 12, 13	1" x 3½"

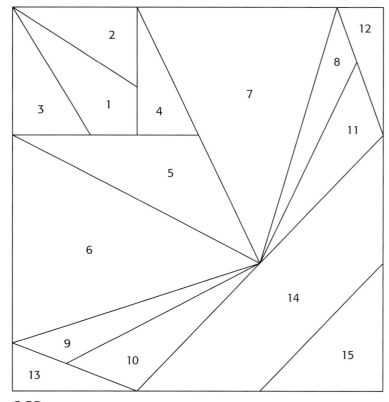

162

Four-Inch Blocks ❈ 105

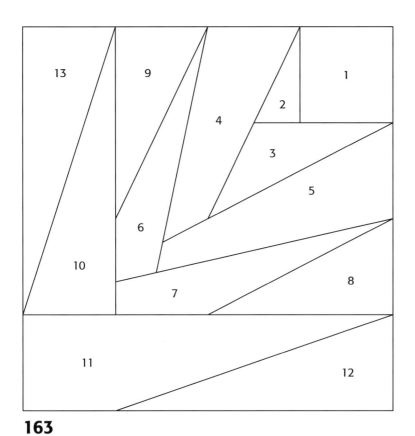

163

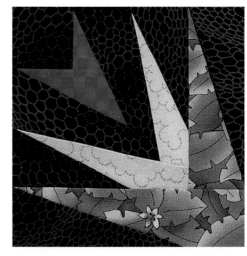

Block 163 Cutting List

Location	Size to Cut
10, 11	1¾" x 4¾"
1	1¾" x 1¾"
4, 5, 8, 9, 12, 13	1½" x 4"
3	1½" x 2½"
6, 7	1¼" x 4"
2	1" x 1¾"

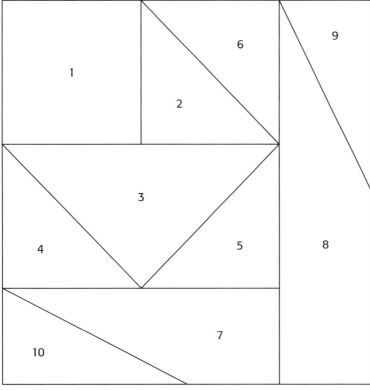

164

Block 164 Cutting List

Location	Size to Cut
3	4½" x 4½" ⊠
2, 4, 5, 6	2¾" x 2¾" ◺
1	2¼" x 2¼"
8	1¾" x 4¾"
7	1¾" x 3¾"
9, 10	1½" x 3½"

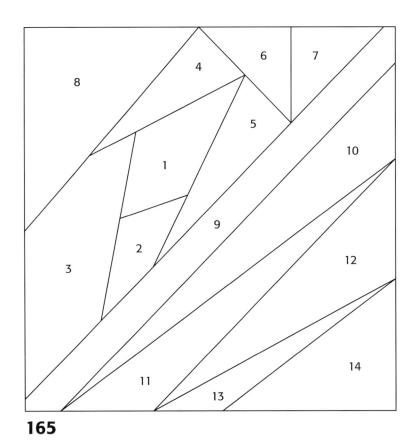

165

Block 165 Cutting List	
Location	**Size to Cut**
8	3¼" x 3¼" ◻
6, 7	2¼" x 2¼" ◻
14	1¾" x 3½"
12, 13	1½" x 4½"
3	1½" x 3¾"
1, 2	1½" x 2½"
9, 10, 11	1¼" x 6½"
4, 5	1¼" x 3"

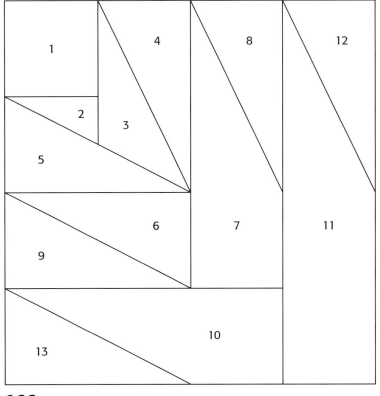

166

Block 166 Cutting List	
Location	**Size to Cut**
11	1¾" x 4¾"
7, 10	1¾" x 3¾"
6	1¾" x 2¾"
1	1¾" x 1¾"
3, 4, 5, 8, 9, 12, 13	1½" x 3"
2	1" x 1½"

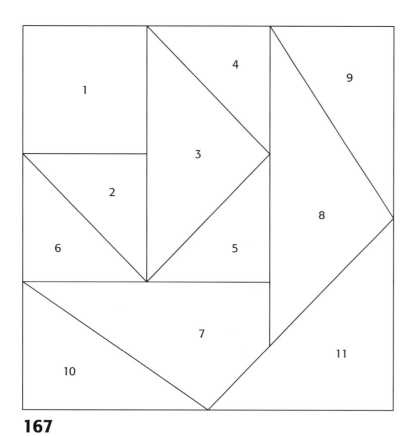

167

Block 167 Cutting List	
Location	**Size to Cut**
3	4¼" x 4¼" ⊠
11	3¼" x 3¼" ◺
2, 4, 5, 6	2¾" x 2¾" ◺
7, 8	2" x 4"
1	2" x 2"
9, 10	1¾" x 3½"

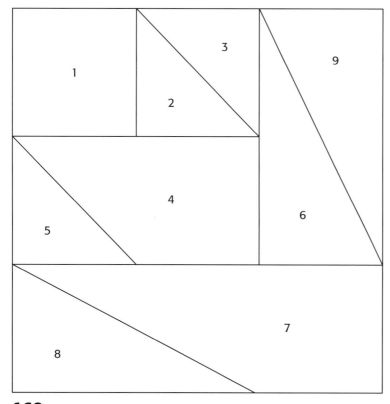

168

Block 168 Cutting List	
Location	**Size to Cut**
2, 3, 5	2¾" x 2¾" ◺
7	2" x 4¾"
4, 6	2" x 3¼"
1	2" x 2"
8, 9	1¾" x 4¼"

Block 169 Cutting List

Location	Size to Cut
1	2" x 2"
6, 11, 16, 21	1¾" x 1¾" ◱
18, 19, 20	1¼" x 5¼"
12, 17	1¼" x 4"
8, 9, 10, 13, 14, 15	1¼" x 3½"
2, 3, 4, 5, 7	1¼" x 2½"

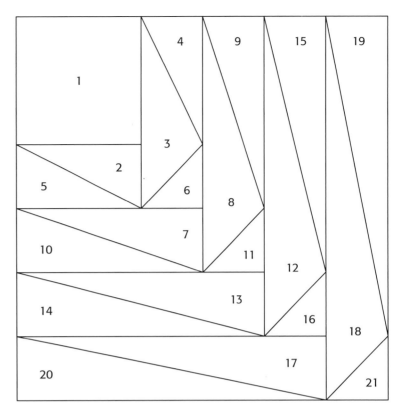

169

Block 170 Cutting List

Location	Size to Cut
2, 3, 4, 5	3" x 3" ⊠
1	2¼" x 2¼"
10	2¼" x 2¼" ◱
6, 9	2" x 5¼"
7, 8	1¾" x 2¾"

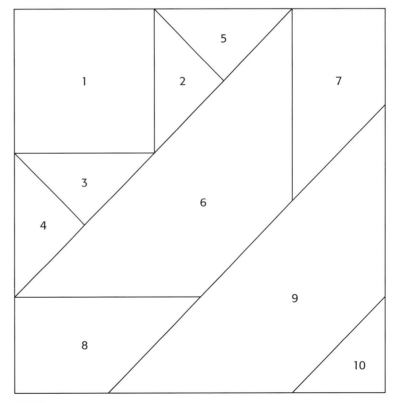

170

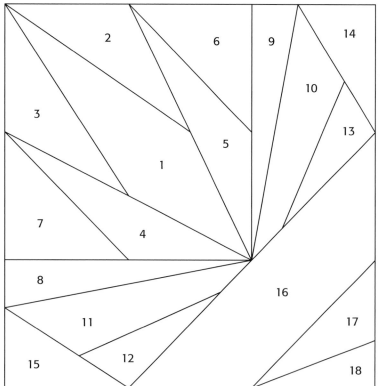

171

Block 171 Cutting List	
Location	**Size to Cut**
6, 7	2¾" x 2¾" ◺
1, 16	1½" x 5"
2, 3, 14, 15	1½" x 3"
4, 5	1¼" x 4¾"
10, 11, 17	1¼" x 3½"
8, 9	1" x 3½"
12, 13, 18	1 x 2½"

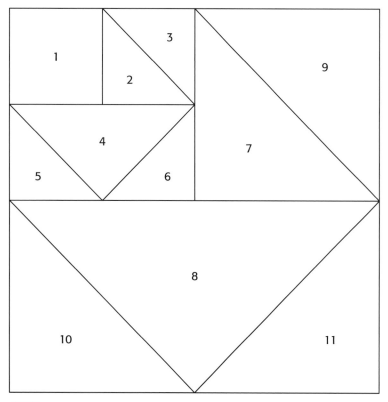

172

Block 172 Cutting List	
Location	**Size to Cut**
8	5½" x 5½" ⊠
4	3½" x 3½" ⊠
7, 9, 10, 11	3¼" x 3¼" ◺
2, 3, 5, 6	2¼" x 2¼" ⊠
1	1¾" x 1¾"

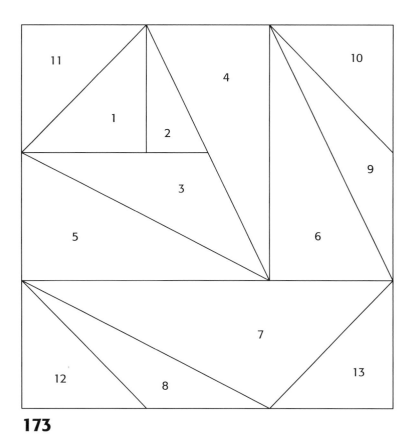

Block 173 Cutting List

Location	Size to Cut
1, 10, 11, 12, 13	2¾" x 2¾" ◺
7	2" x 4¾"
3, 6	2" x 3½"
4, 5	1¾" x 4"
8, 9	1¼" x 4"
2	1¼" x 2"

173

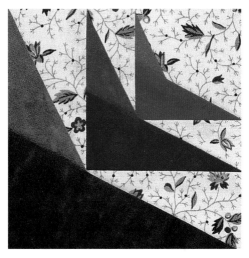

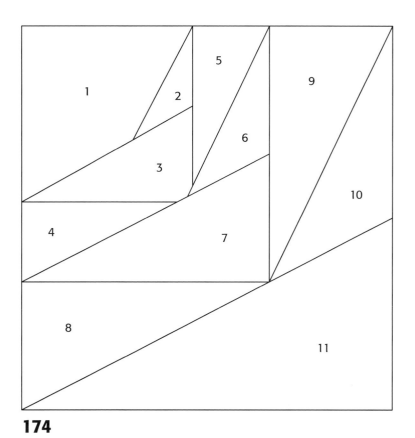

Block 174 Cutting List

Location	Size to Cut
11	2½" x 5½"
1	2½" x 2½"
8, 9	2" x 3½"
7	1¾" x 4"
10	1½" x 3¾"
3, 4, 5	1½" x 3"
6	1¼" x 3"
2	1" x 2"

174

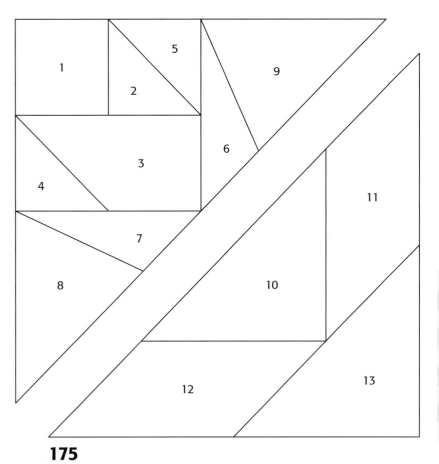

175

Block 175 Cutting List	
Location	**Size to Cut**
10, 13	3¼" x 3¼" ◹
8, 9	2½" x 2½"
2, 4, 5	2¼" x 2¼" ◹
11, 12	1¾" x 3¾"
3	1¾" x 2¾"
1	1¾" x 1¾"
6, 7	1¼" x 2¾"

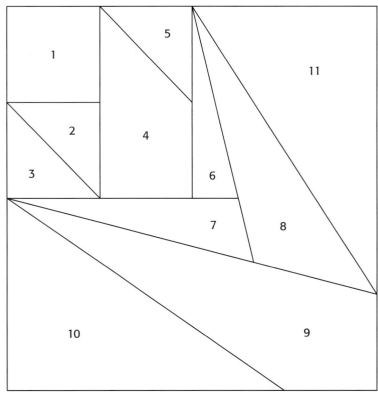

176

Block 176 Cutting List	
Location	**Size to Cut**
10, 11	2¼" x 4¾"
2, 3, 5	2¼" x 2¼" ◹
9	2" x 5¼"
8	2" x 4¼"
4	1¾" x 2¾"
1	1¾" x 1¾"
7	1¼" x 3½"
6	1¼" x 2¾"

Block 177 Cutting List

Location	Size to Cut
1	2¾" x 3¾"
5	2½" x 4½"
4	2" x 4½"
6	1½" x 5"
2, 3	1½" x 3"

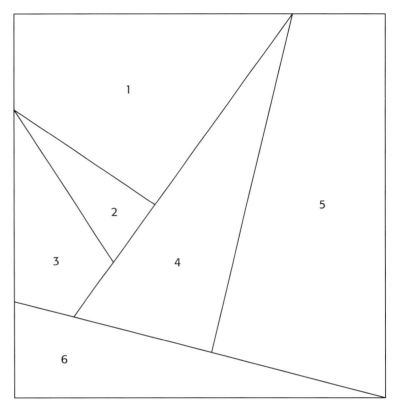

177

Block 178 Cutting List

Location	Size to Cut
3, 4, 7	2½" x 4½"
5	1¾" x 5¼"
6	1¾" x 3¼"
1	1¾" x 2¾"
2	1¼" x 2"

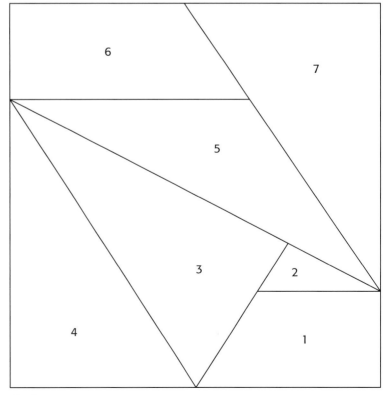

178

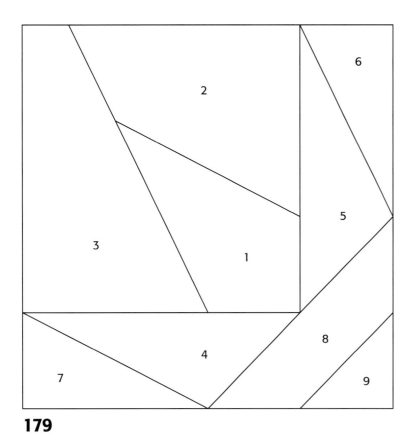

179

Block 179 Cutting List	
Location	**Size to Cut**
2, 3	2¼" x 4¼"
9	2¼" x 2¼" ◹
1	2" x 3½"
4, 5	1¾" x 3½"
6, 7	1½" x 3"
8	1¼" x 4"

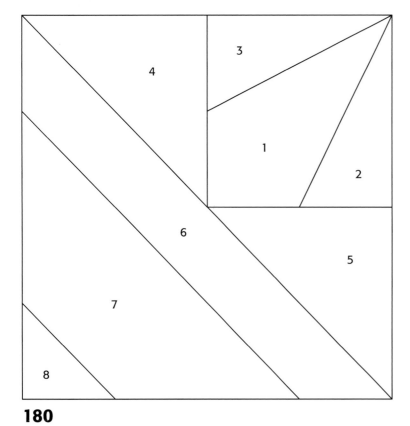

180

Block 180 Cutting List	
Location	**Size to Cut**
4, 5	3¼" x 3¼" ◹
8	2¼" x 2¼" ◹
7	2" x 5¼"
1	2" x 3½"
6	1½" x 6½"
2, 3	1½" x 3"

Block 181 Cutting List

Location	Size to Cut
6, 7	3¼" x 3¼" ◻
1	2" x 5"
2, 3	1¾" x 2¾"
4, 5	1½" x 5"

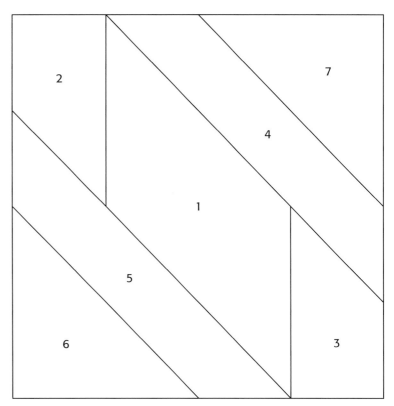

181

Block 182 Cutting List

Location	Size to Cut
1	3¾" x 3¾"
6	3¼" x 3¼" ◻
4, 5	1¾" x 3¾"
2, 3	1½" x 4"

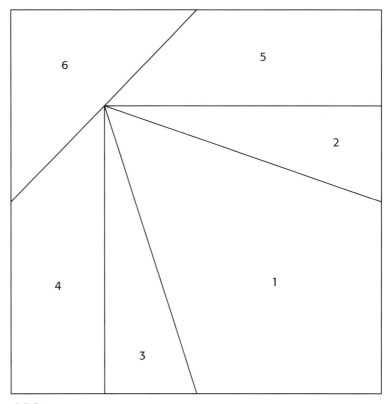

182

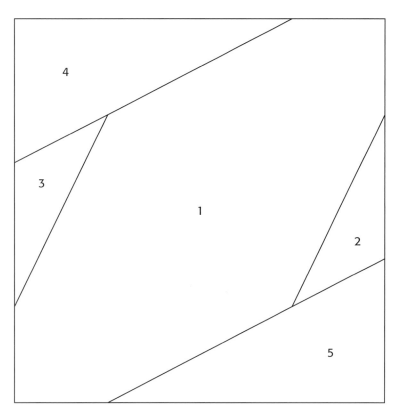

183

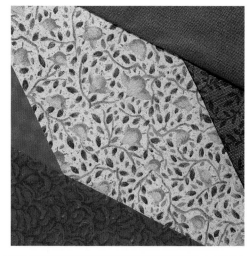

Block 183 Cutting List	
Location	Size to Cut
1	3½" x 6½"
4, 5	2" x 4½"
2, 3	1¼" x 3¼"

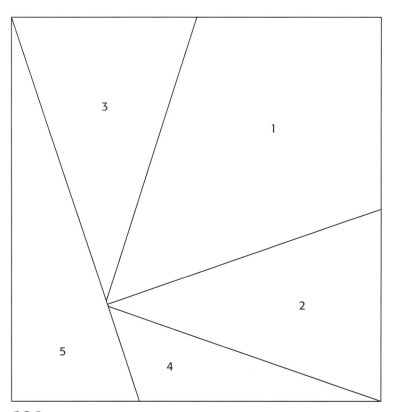

184

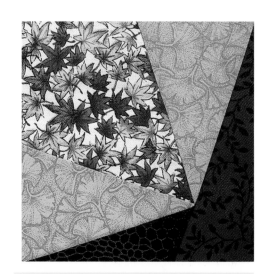

Block 184 Cutting List	
Location	Size to Cut
1	3¾" x 3¾"
2, 3	2½" x 3¾"
5	2" x 5"
4	1½" x 3¾"

Block 185 Cutting List

Location	Size to Cut
1	3½" x 3½"
6	3¼" x 3¼" ◻
4, 5	2½" x 3¾"
3	2¼" x 2¼" ◻
2	1¼" x 4"

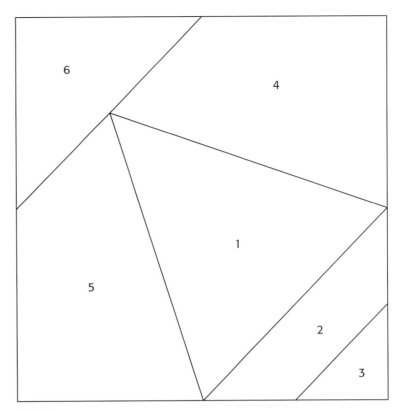

185

Block 186 Cutting List

Location	Size to Cut
2, 3	3" x 3½"
5	2" x 5½"
1	2" x 3½"
6	1¾" x 4"
4	1½" x 6½"

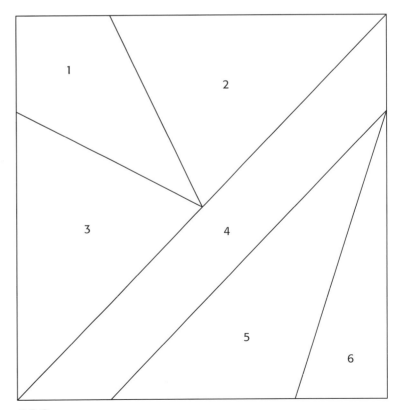

186

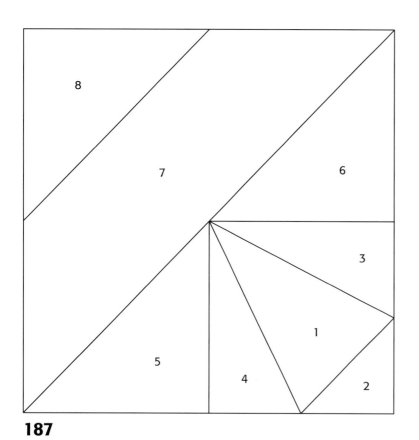

187

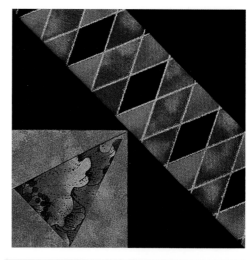

Block 187 Cutting List	
Location	**Size to Cut**
5, 6, 8	3¼" x 3¼" ◺
2	2¼" x 2¼" ◺
7	2" x 6½"
1	2" x 2¾"
3, 4	1½" x 3"

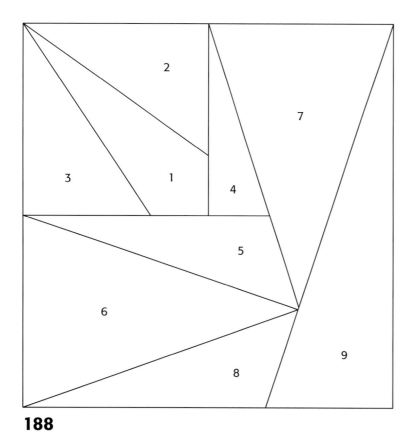

188

Block 188 Cutting List	
Location	**Size to Cut**
6, 7	2½" x 4"
9	2" x 5"
5	1¾" x 3½"
8	1½" x 3¾"
1, 2, 3	1½" x 3½"
4	1¼" x 2¾"

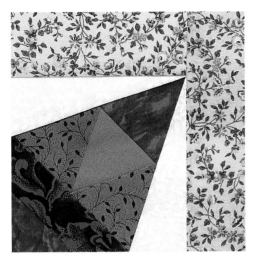

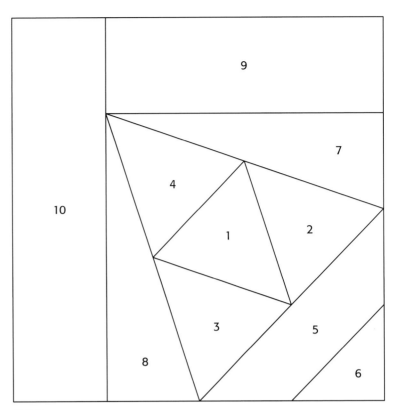

189

Block 189 Cutting List

Location	Size to Cut
6	2¼" x 2¼" ◺
1, 2, 3, 4	2" x 2"
10	1¾" x 4¾"
9	1¾" x 3¾"
7, 8	1½" x 4"
5	1¼" x 3¾"

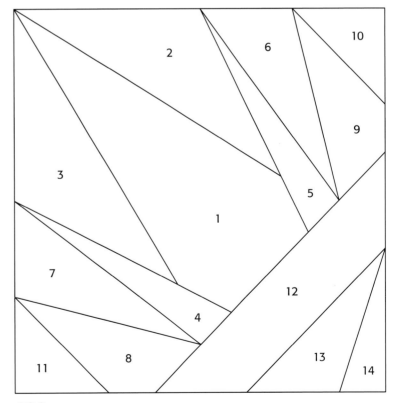

190

Block 190 Cutting List

Location	Size to Cut
1	2¼" x 4¾"
10, 11	2¼" x 2¼" ◺
2, 3	1¾" x 4"
6, 7	1½" x 3¼"
8, 9, 14	1½" x 2½"
12	1¼" x 4½"
13	1¼" x 3¼"
4, 5	1" x 3¼"

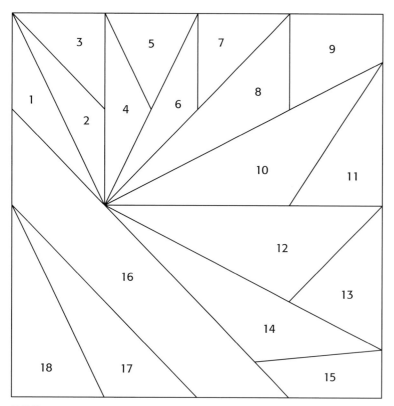

191

Block 191 Cutting List	
Location	**Size to Cut**
3, 7	2¼" x 2¼" ◹
12, 13	1¾" x 3½"
9	1¾" x 1¾"
10, 16	1½" x 5"
5, 11, 18	1½" x 3"
14, 17	1¼" x 4¼"
1, 2, 4, 6, 8	1¼" x 3½"
15	1¼" x 2¼"

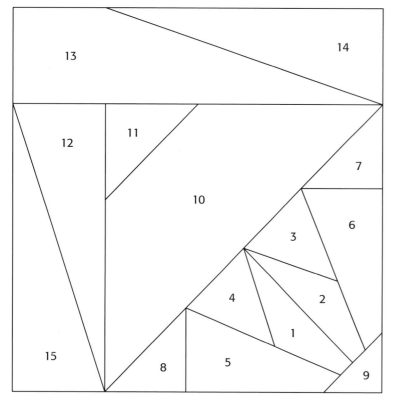

192

Block 192 Cutting List	
Location	**Size to Cut**
7, 8, 9, 11	2¼" x 2¼" ◹
10	2" x 5"
13	1¾" x 4¾"
12	1¾" x 3¾"
14, 15	1½" x 4"
5, 6	1½" x 2½"
3, 4	1½" x 1¾"
1, 2	1" x 2½"

Block 193 Cutting List

Location	Size to Cut
7, 8, 9	3¼" x 3¼" ◺
1	2¾" x 2¾"
5	1¾" x 4¾"
6	1¾" x 3¾"
3, 4	1¾" x 2½"
2	1" x 2¾"

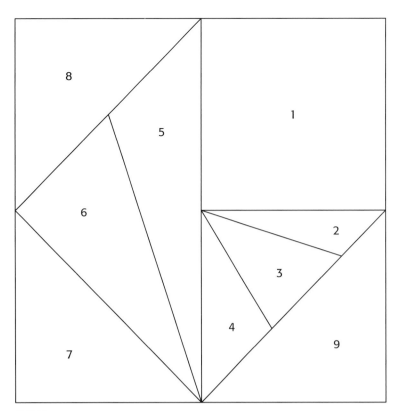

193

Block 194 Cutting List

Location	Size to Cut
17	2½" x 2½" ◺
2, 7, 8, 9, 14, 15	2¼" x 2¼" ◺
1	2" x 3½"
3, 4	1½" x 3½"
5, 6, 10, 11, 16	1¼" x 3½"
12, 13	1¼" x 2½"

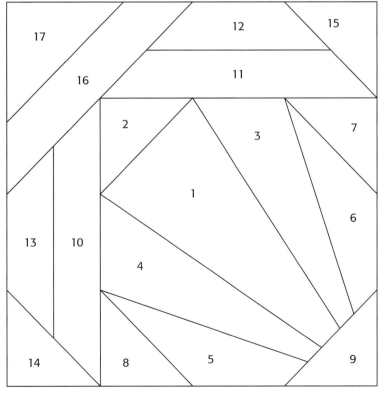

194

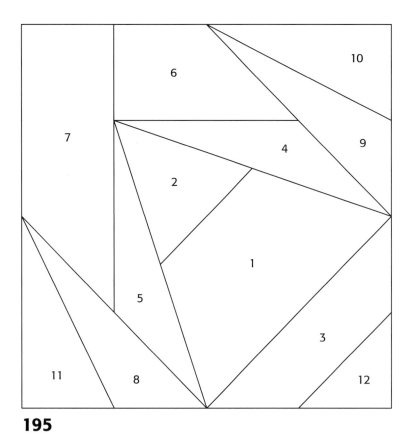

195

Block 195 Cutting List	
Location	**Size to Cut**
12	2¼" x 2¼" ◨
1	2" x 3½"
2	2" x 2¼"
7	1¾" x 3¾"
6	1¾" x 2¾"
10, 11	1½" x 3"
3, 4, 5, 8, 9	1¼" x 4"

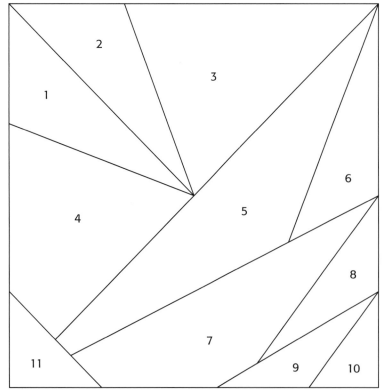

196

Block 196 Cutting List	
Location	**Size to Cut**
3, 4	3" x 3¼"
11	2¼" x 2¼" ◨
5	1¾" x 5¾"
7	1¾" x 4½"
1, 2	1½" x 3½"
6, 8	1¼" x 3½"
10	1¼" x 3"
9	1" x 3"

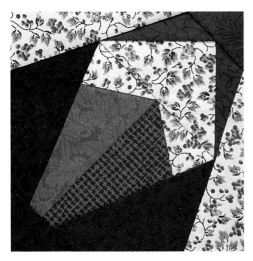

Block 197 Cutting List

Location	Size to Cut
5	3¼" x 3¼" ◨
8, 13	2¼" x 2¼" ◨
1, 2, 9, 10	1¾" x 3¾"
11, 12	1½" x 4¼"
3, 4	1½" x 2"
6, 7	1" x 2½"

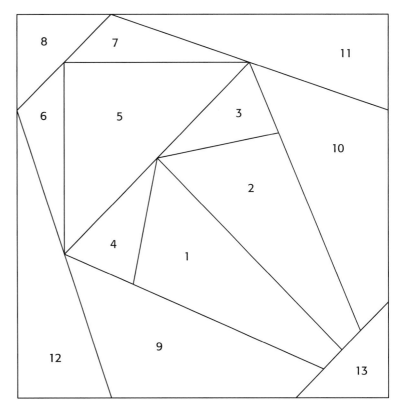

197

Block 198 Cutting List

Location	Size to Cut
1	2½" x 4¼"
10, 11	2¼" x 2¼" ◨
2, 3, 14	1½" x 3¾"
8, 9	1½" x 2½"
12	1¼" x 5¼"
13	1¼" x 4"
4, 5, 6, 7	1¼" x 3"

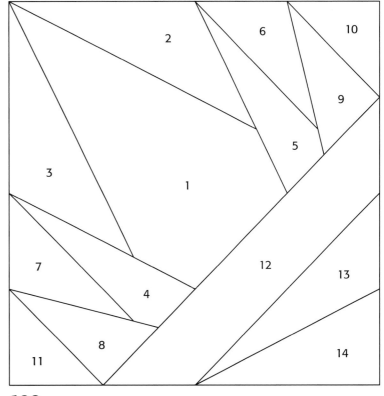

198

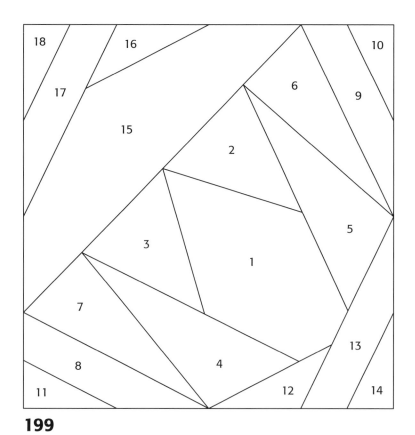

199

Block 199 Cutting List	
Location	**Size to Cut**
1	2¼" x 3¼"
15	1¾" x 5¼"
4, 5	1½" x 3¼"
6, 7	1½" x 2¾"
2, 3	1½" x 2¼"
10, 11, 14, 18	1¼" x 2½"
8, 9, 12, 13, 16, 17	1" x 3½"

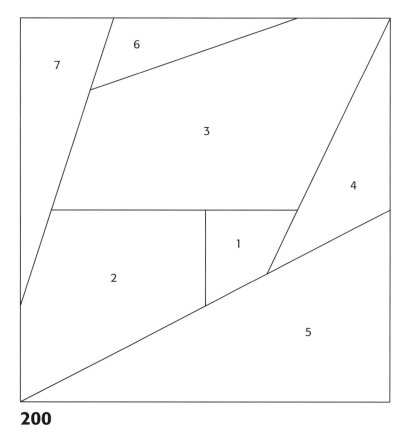

200

Block 200 Cutting List	
Location	**Size to Cut**
3	2¾" x 4½"
2	2¾" x 2¾"
5	2½" x 5½"
1	1¾" x 1¾"
4, 7	1½" x 4"
6	1¼" x 3¼"

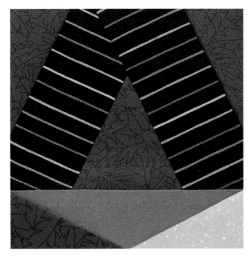

Block 201 Cutting List

Location	Size to Cut
1	2¾" x 2¾"
2, 3	2" x 4½"
6	1¾" x 4¾"
4, 5, 7, 8	1½" x 3½"

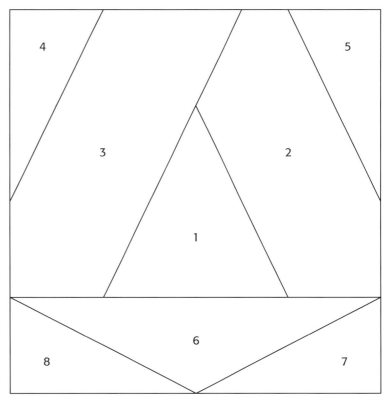

201

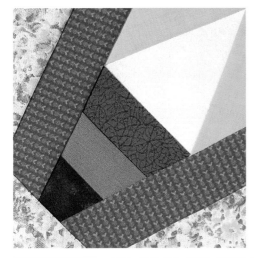

Block 202 Cutting List

Location	Size to Cut
1	3" x 3"
11	2½" x 2½" ◺
7, 8	1½" x 4½"
9, 10	1½" x 3½"
2, 3	1½" x 2¾"
4	1½" x 1¾"
5, 6	1¼" x 3¼"

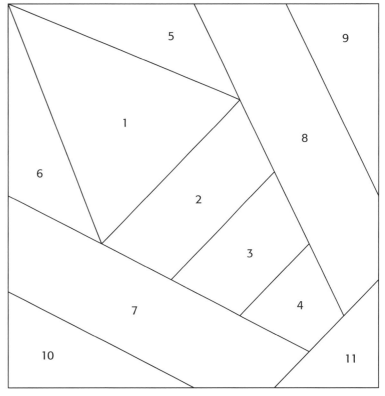

202

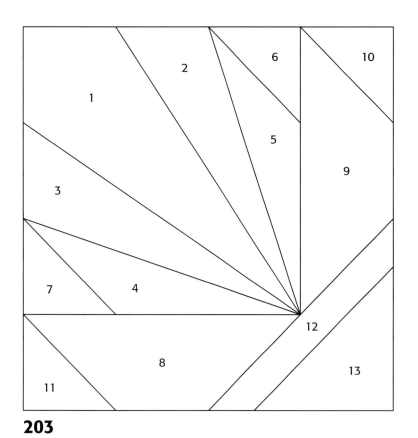

203

Block 203 Cutting List	
Location	**Size to Cut**
13	2¾" x 2¾" ◺
6, 7, 10, 11	2¼" x 2¼" ◺
1	2" x 5"
8, 9	1¾" x 3¾"
2, 3	1½" x 4½"
4, 5, 12	1¼" x 4"

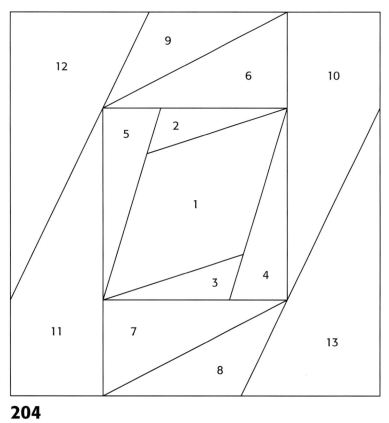

204

Block 204 Cutting List	
Location	**Size to Cut**
1	2¾" x 2¾"
12, 13	2" x 4½"
10, 11	1¾" x 3¾"
6, 7	1¾" x 2¾"
4, 5, 8, 9	1¼" x 3"
2, 3	1" x 2½"

Block 205 Cutting List

Location	Size to Cut
6	3¼" x 3¼" ◨
1	2" x 3½"
8	1¾" x 4¾"
7	1¾" x 3¾"
2, 3, 9, 10	1½" x 3¼"
4, 5	1½" x 2½"

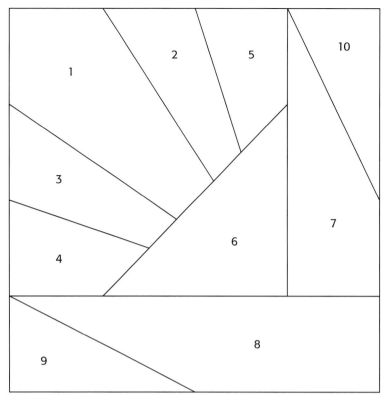

205

Block 206 Cutting List

Location	Size to Cut
1	3½" x 4"
2, 3	1¾" x 4½"
5	1½" x 3½"
7	1¼" x 4¾"
4, 6	1¼" x 4"

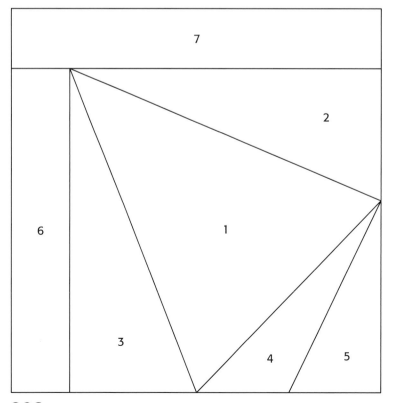

206

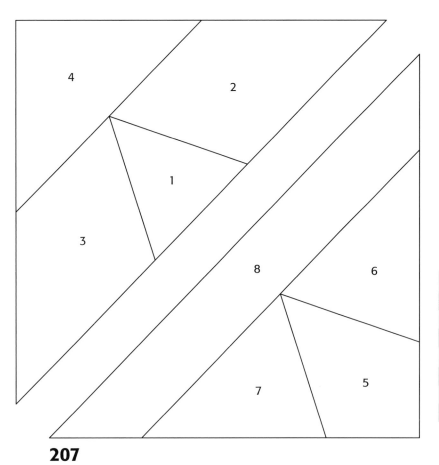

207

Block 207 Cutting List

Location	Size to Cut
4	3¼" x 3¼" ◻
2, 3	2½" x 3½"
6, 7	2½" x 2½"
5	2¼" x 2¼"
1	2" x 2"
8	1½" x 6½"

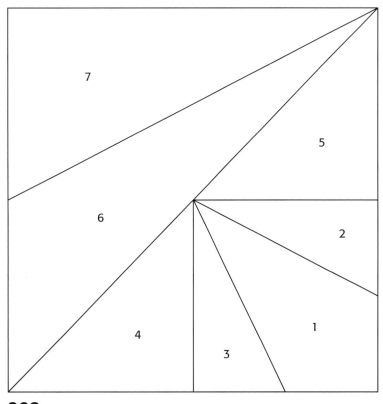

208

Block 208 Cutting List

Location	Size to Cut
4, 5	3¼" x 3¼" ◻
1	2¾" x 2¾"
7	2½" x 5½"
6	2" x 6½"
2, 3	1¾" x 3"

Block 209 Cutting List

Location	Size to Cut
3, 4, 5	3½" x 3½" ⊠
7	3¼" x 3¼" ◺
2, 10, 11	2¼" x 2¼" ◺
9	1¾" x 4¾"
8	1¾" x 3¾"
1	1¾" x 1¾"
6	1½" x 5"

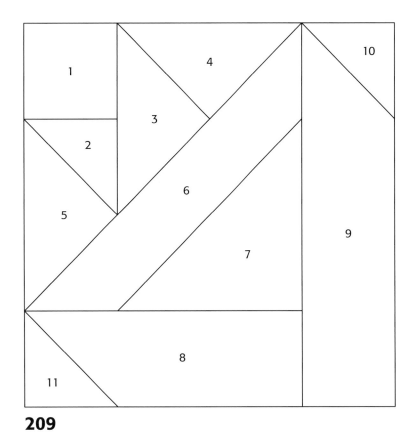

209

Block 210 Cutting List

Location	Size to Cut
10, 11	3¾" x 3¾" ◺
1	2¼" x 2¼"
3	1¾" x 3¼"
2	1¾" x 2¼"
6, 7, 8, 9	1¼" x 2¾"
4, 5	1" x 2¾"

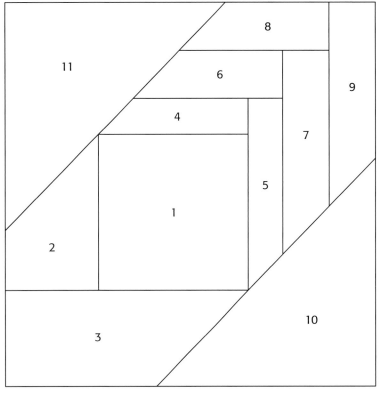

210

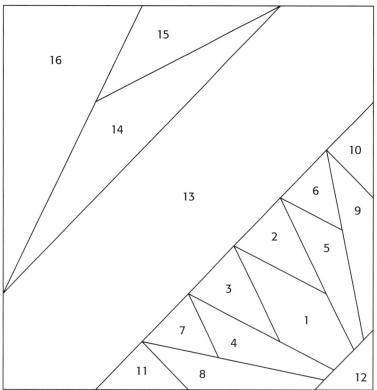

211

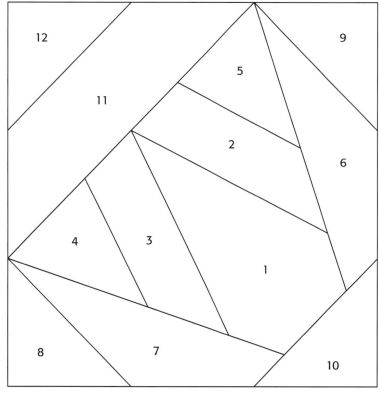

212

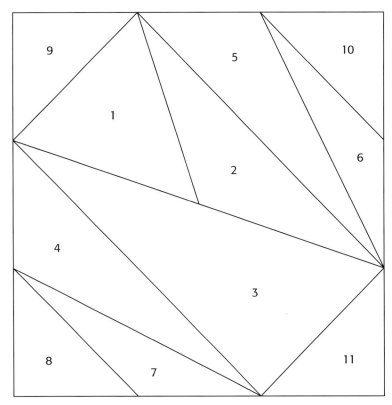

Block 213 Cutting List

Location	Size to Cut
8, 9, 10, 11	2¾" x 2¾" ◺
2	2½" x 4"
1	2½" x 2½"
3	2¼" x 5"
4, 5	1½" x 4½"
6, 7	1¼" x 4"

213

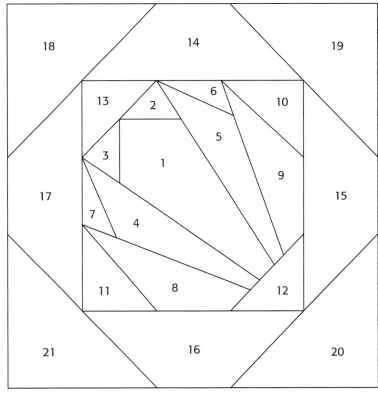

Block 214 Cutting List

Location	Size to Cut
18, 19, 20, 21	3" x 3" ◺
12, 13	2" x 2" ◺
14, 15, 16, 17	1½" x 3¼"
1	1½" x 2¾"
8, 9	1¼" x 2¾"
10, 11	1¼" x 2"
4, 5	1" x 3"
2, 3, 6, 7	1" x 1½"

214

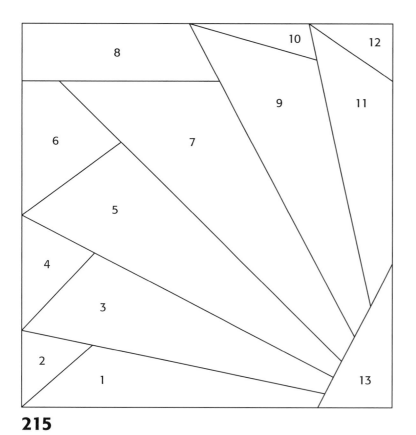

215

Block 215 Cutting List

Location	Size to Cut
5, 7, 9	1¾" x 5"
6	1¾" x 2"
3	1½" x 4"
13	1½" x 3"
4	1½" x 2"
1, 11	1¼" x 4"
8	1¼" x 2¾"
2, 10, 12	1¼" x 2"

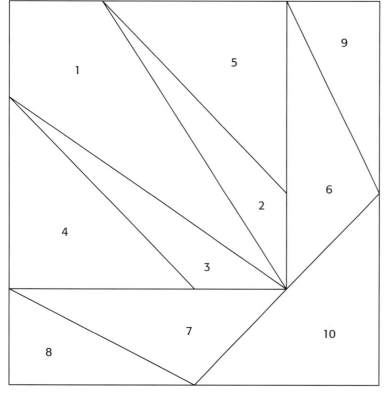

216

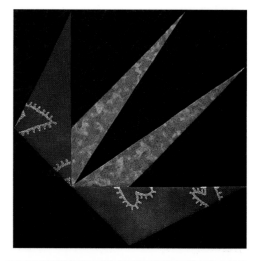

Block 216 Cutting List

Location	Size to Cut
4, 5, 10	3¼" x 3¼" ◻
1	2" x 5"
6, 7	1¾" x 3¾"
8, 9	1½" x 3¾"
2, 3	1¼" x 4½"

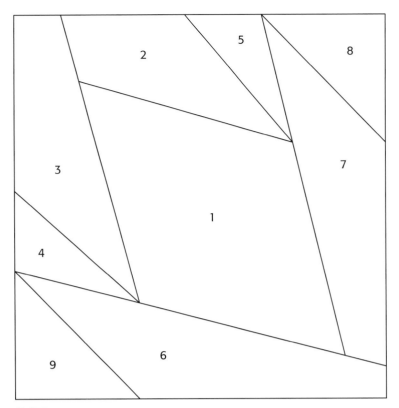

Block 217 Cutting List

Location	Size to Cut
1	3" x 4½"
8, 9	2¾" x 2¾" ◻
6, 7	1¾" x 5"
2, 3	1½" x 4"
4, 5	1¼" x 2½"

217

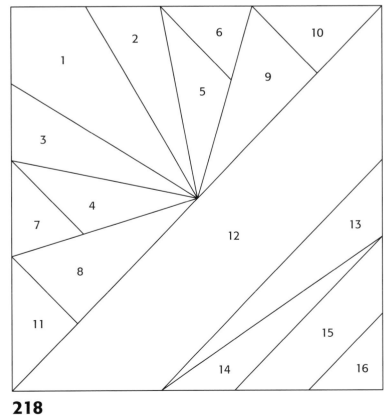

Block 218 Cutting List

Location	Size to Cut
10, 11, 16	2¼" x 2¼" ◻
12	1¾" x 6½"
1	1¾" x 3½"
8, 9	1½" x 2¾"
13	1¼" x 4½"
14, 15	1¼" x 3¾"
2, 3, 4, 5	1¼" x 3"
6, 7	1¼" x 2"

218

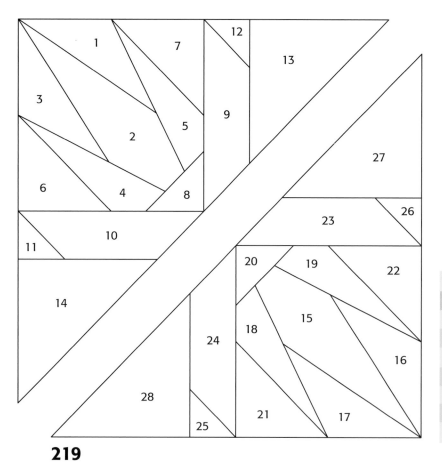

219

Block 219 Cutting List	
Location	**Size to Cut**
13, 14, 27, 28	2¾" x 2¾" ◺
6, 7, 21, 22	2¼" x 2¼" ◺
8, 20	2" x 2" ◺
11, 12, 25, 26	1¾" x 1¾" ◺
1, 15	1¼" x 3"
9, 10, 23, 24	1¼" x 2½"
2, 3, 4, 5, 16, 17, 18, 19	1" x 2½"

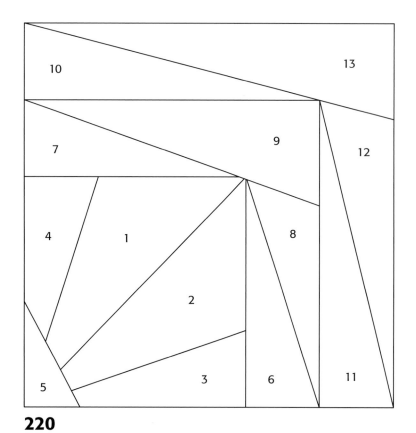

220

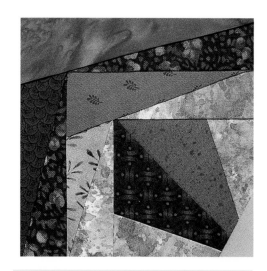

Block 220 Cutting List	
Location	**Size to Cut**
13	1¾" x 4¾"
9	1¾" x 4¼"
1, 2	1¾" x 3½"
10, 11, 12	1½" x 4"
6, 7, 8	1½" x 3¼"
3, 4, 5	1¼" x 2½"

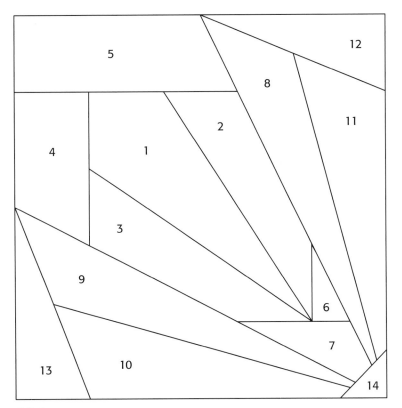

Block 221 Cutting List

Location	Size to Cut
1	2" x 4"
14	1¾" x 1¾" ◺
10, 11	1½" x 4"
5, 12, 13	1½" x 3"
4	1½" x 2¼"
8, 9	1¼" x 5"
2, 3	1¼" x 3½"
6, 7	1¼" x 2"

221

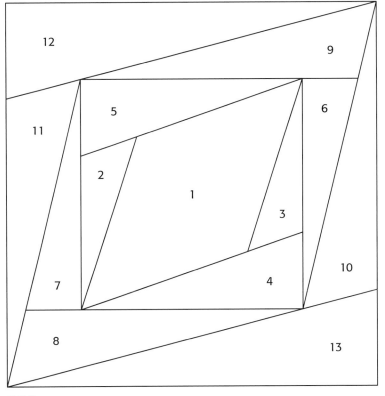

Block 222 Cutting List

Location	Size to Cut
1	2½" x 4"
12, 13	1¾" x 5"
8, 9, 10, 11	1½" x 4"
4, 5	1¼" x 3¼"
6, 7	1¼" x 3"
2, 3	1¼" x 2½"

222

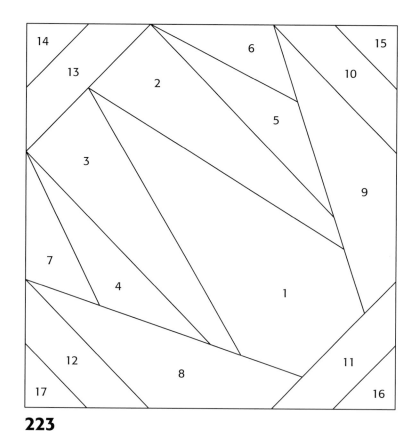

223

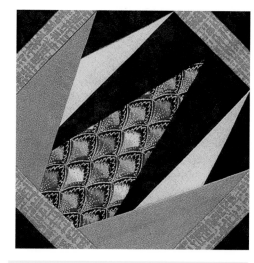

Block 223 Cutting List	
Location	**Size to Cut**
1	2¼" x 4½"
14, 15, 16, 17	2" x 2" ◺
2, 3, 8, 9	1½" x 4"
4, 5	1¼" x 3½"
6, 7	1¼" x 2½"
10, 11, 12, 13	1" x 3"

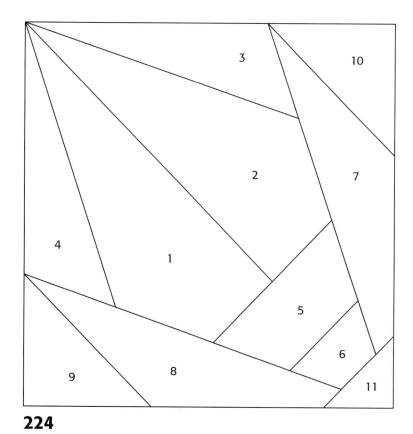

224

Block 224 Cutting List	
Location	**Size to Cut**
9, 10	2¾" x 2¾" ◺
1, 2	2" x 4½"
11	2" x 2" ◺
7, 8	1½" x 4½"
3, 4	1½" x 3¾"
5	1½" x 2½"
6	1¼" x 2"

Block 225 Cutting List

Location	Size to Cut
6	2¼" x 3¼"
11	2" x 5"
2, 4, 8, 10	1¾" x 3"
1	1½" x 3½"
3, 5	1¼" x 3½"
7, 9	1¼" x 5"

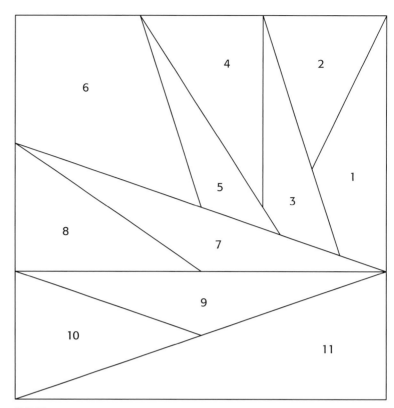

225

Block 226 Cutting List

Location	Size to Cut
16	2¾" x 2¾" ◺
1, 2, 8, 9	2¼" x 2¼" ◺
3	1¾" x 2¾"
11	1½" x 6½"
13, 15	1¼" x 5"
4, 5, 14	1¼" x 3"
10, 12	1" x 6"
6, 7	1" x 2¼"

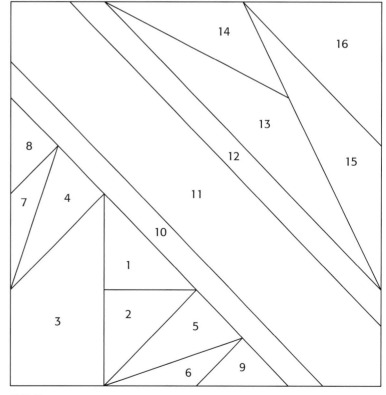

226

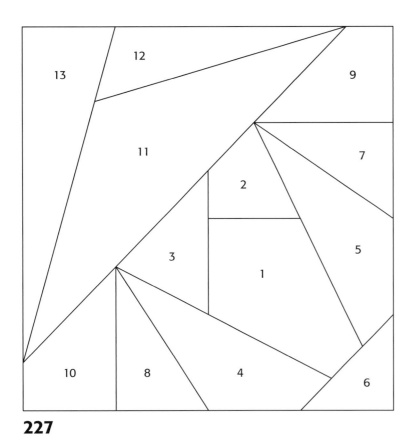

227

Block 227 Cutting List	
Location	**Size to Cut**
6	2¼" x 2¼" ◱
11	2" x 6"
1	2" x 2¾"
9, 10	1¾" x 2¼"
13	1½" x 4½"
4, 5, 12	1½" x 3½"
3, 7, 8	1½" x 2½"
2	1½" x 1¾"

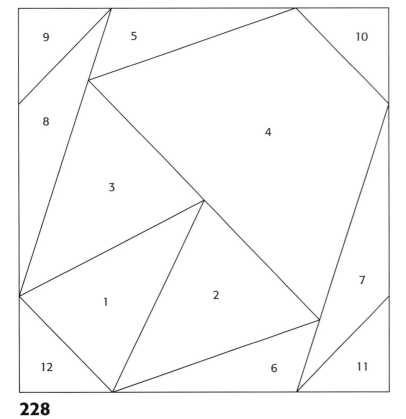

228

Block 228 Cutting List	
Location	**Size to Cut**
4	2¾" x 4¼"
2, 3	2¼" x 3"
9, 10, 11, 12	2¼" x 2¼" ◱
1	2" x 2¾"
7, 8	1¼" x 4"
5, 6	1¼" x 3¼"

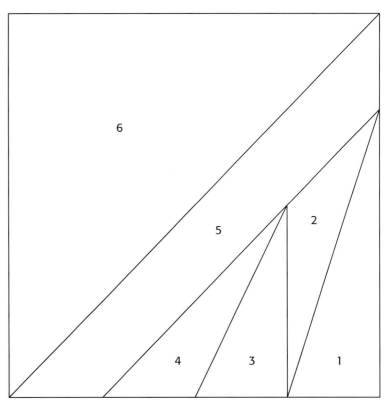

Block 229 Cutting List

Location	Size to Cut
6	$5\frac{1}{4}$" x $5\frac{1}{4}$" ◹
1	$1\frac{3}{4}$" x $3\frac{3}{4}$"
3, 4	$1\frac{1}{2}$" x $3\frac{1}{4}$"
5	$1\frac{1}{4}$" x $6\frac{1}{2}$"
2	$1\frac{1}{4}$" x 4"

229

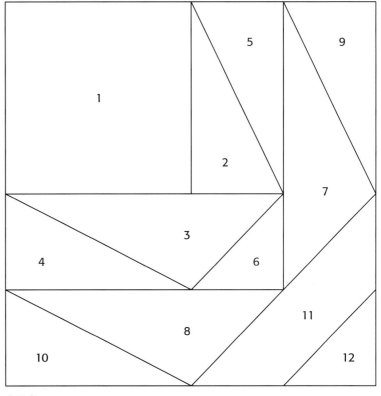

Block 230 Cutting List

Location	Size to Cut
1	$2\frac{3}{4}$" x $2\frac{3}{4}$"
6, 12	$2\frac{1}{4}$" x $2\frac{1}{4}$" ◹
3, 7, 8	$1\frac{3}{4}$" x $3\frac{3}{4}$"
2	$1\frac{3}{4}$" x $2\frac{3}{4}$"
4, 5, 9, 10	$1\frac{1}{2}$" x 3"
11	$1\frac{1}{4}$" x 4"

230

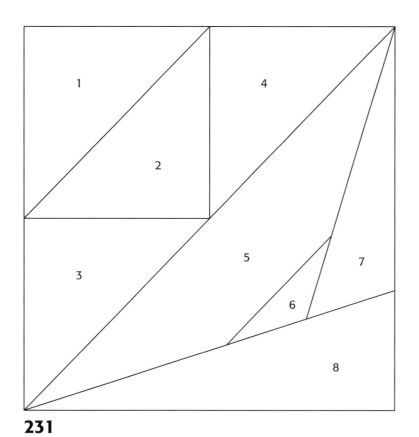

231

Block 231 Cutting List	
Location	**Size to Cut**
1, 2, 3, 4	3¼" x 3¼" ◺
5	1¾" x 6½"
8	1¾" x 5"
7	1½" x 4"
6	1" x 2½"

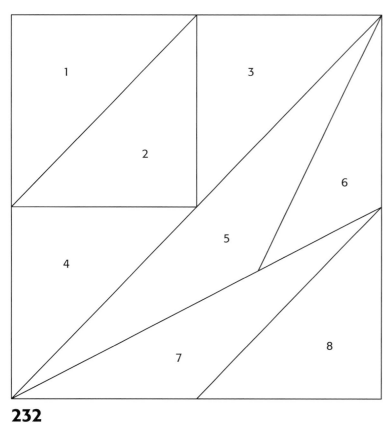

232

Block 232 Cutting List	
Location	**Size to Cut**
1, 2, 3, 4, 8	3¼" x 3¼" ◺
5	1½" x 6½"
7	1½" x 5½"
6	1½" x 3¾"

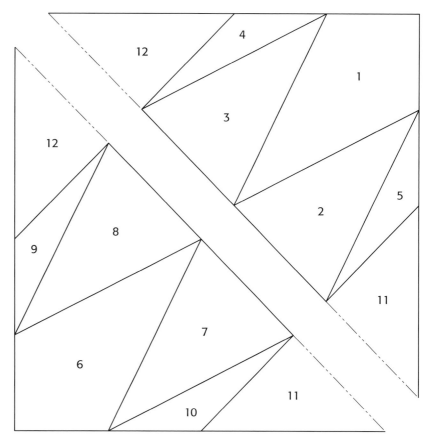

233

Block 233 Cutting List

Location	Size to Cut
11, 12	3¼" x 3¼" ◺
1, 6	2" x 3½"
2, 3, 7, 8	2" x 3"
4, 5, 9, 10	1" x 3"

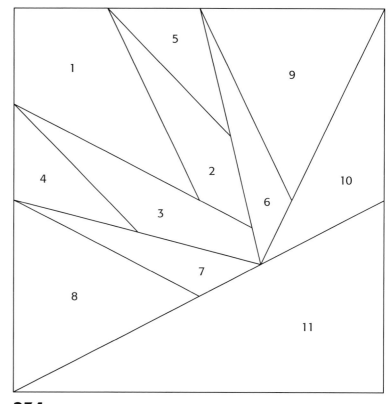

234

Block 234 Cutting List

Location	Size to Cut
11	2½" x 5½"
8, 9	2½" x 3"
1	2" x 3"
10	1½" x 3¾"
2, 3	1¼" x 3¾"
4, 5	1¼" x 2¾"
6, 7	1" x 3½"

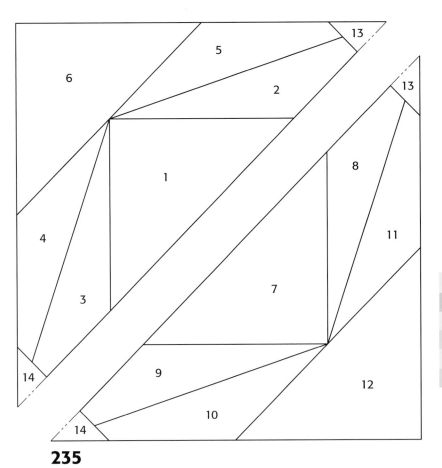

235

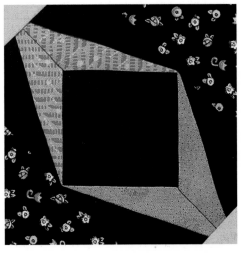

Block 235 Cutting List	
Location	**Size to Cut**
1, 6, 7, 12	3¼" x 3¼" ◻
13, 14	2" x 2" ◻
2, 3, 8, 9	1½" x 3½"
4, 5, 10, 11	1¼" x 3½"

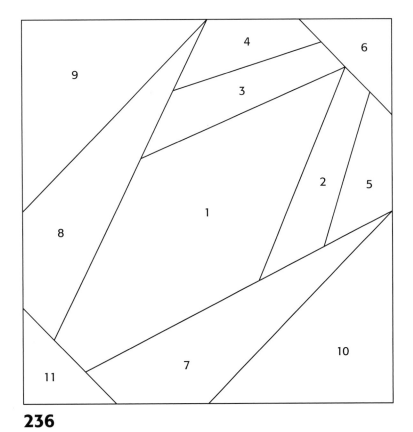

236

Block 236 Cutting List	
Location	**Size to Cut**
9, 10	3¼" x 3¼" ◻
1	2½" x 4¾"
6, 11	2¼" x 2¼" ◻
7, 8	1½" x 4½"
2, 3	1¼" x 3"
4, 5	1¼" x 2½"

Block 237 Cutting List

Location	Size to Cut
1, 2, 8, 9	3½" x 3½" ⊠
3, 10	3¼" x 3¼" ◹
6, 7, 13, 14	2¼" x 2¼" ◹
4, 5, 11, 12	1¾" x 2¾"

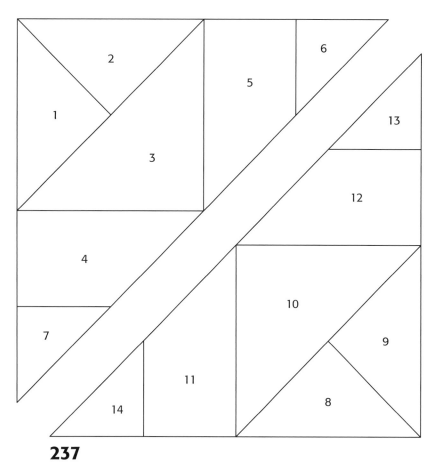

237

Block 238 Cutting List

Location	Size to Cut
2, 3	4¼" x 4¼" ⊠
1	4" x 4" ◹
6, 7, 8, 9	2¾" x 2¾" ◹
4, 5	1½" x 4½"

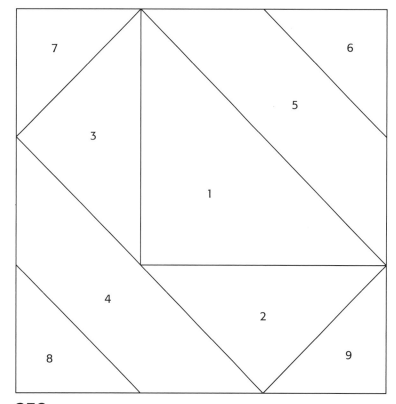

238

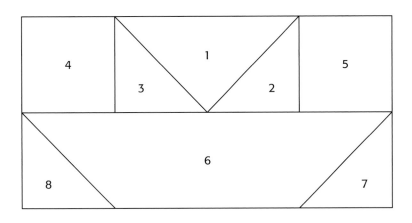

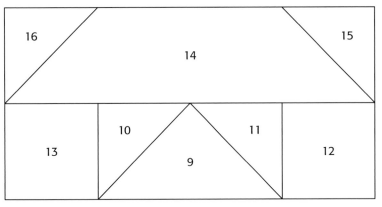

239

Block 239 Cutting List

Location	Size to Cut
1, 9	3½" x 3½" ⊠
2, 3, 7, 8, 10, 11, 15, 16	2¼" x 2¼" ◹
6, 14	1¾" x 4¾"
4, 5, 12, 13	1¾" x 1¾"

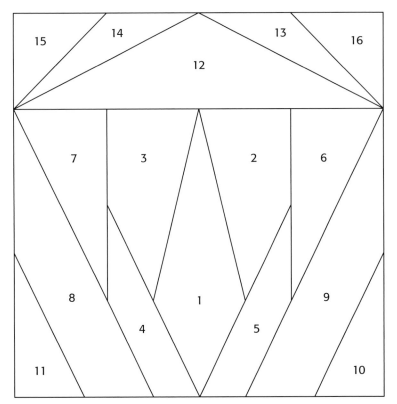

240

Block 240 Cutting List

Location	Size to Cut
15, 16	2¼" x 2¼" ◹
12	1¾" x 4¾"
1	1¾" x 3¾"
6, 7	1¾" x 2¾"
2, 3	1½" x 2¾"
8, 9	1¼" x 4¾"
10, 11	1¼" x 2¾"
4, 5, 13, 14	1" x 3"

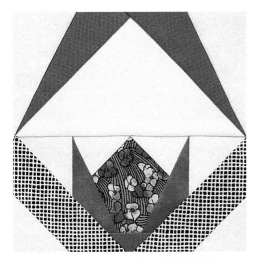

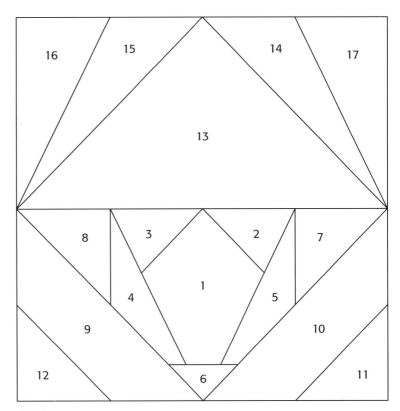

Block 241 Cutting List

Location	Size to Cut
13	5½" x 5½" ⊠
7, 8, 11, 12	2¼" x 2¼" ◨
1	2" x 2¼"
6	1¾" x 1¾" ◺
16, 17	1½" x 3¼"
2, 3	1½" x 1½"
9, 10, 14, 15	1¼" x 3¾"
4, 5	1" x 2½"

241

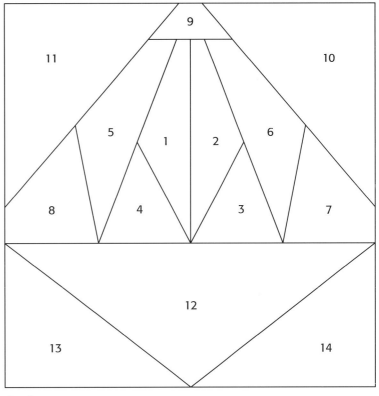

Block 242 Cutting List

Location	Size to Cut
12	2¼" x 4¾"
10, 11	2" x 4"
13, 14	1¾" x 3½"
3, 4, 7, 8	1½" x 2"
1, 2, 5, 6	1¼" x 3"
9	1" x 2"

242

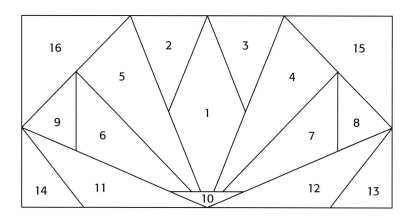

243

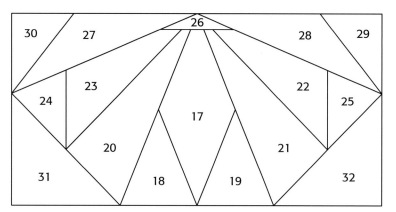

Block 243 Cutting List

Location	Size to Cut
15, 16, 31, 32	2½" x 2½" ◪
1, 4, 5, 17, 20, 21	1½" x 2¾"
6, 7, 22, 23	1¼" x 2½"
13, 14, 29, 30	1¼" x 2"
2, 3, 18, 19	1¼" x 1¾"
8, 9, 24, 25	1¼" x 1½"
11, 12, 27, 28	1" x 3"
10, 26	1" x 1½"

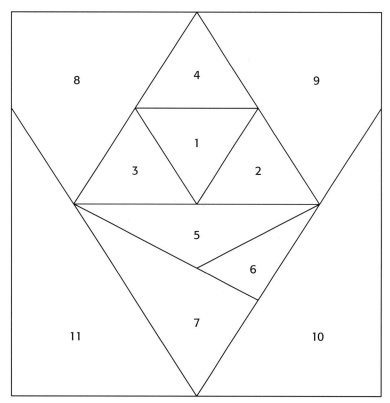

244

Block 244 Cutting List

Location	Size to Cut
10, 11	2¼" x 4¾"
8, 9	2¼" x 3¼"
7	1¾" x 3"
1, 2, 3, 4	1¾" x 2"
5	1¼" x 3½"
6	1¼" x 2½"

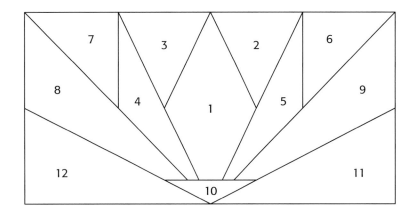

Block 245 Cutting List

Location	Size to Cut
6, 7, 18, 19	2¼" x 2¼" ◹
11, 12, 23, 24	1½" x 3"
1, 13	1½" x 2½"
2, 3, 14, 15	1½" x 2"
8, 9, 20, 21	1¼" x 3"
4, 5, 16, 17	1" x 2½"
10, 22	1" x 2"

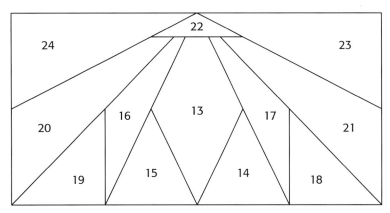

245

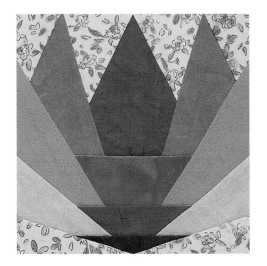

Block 246 Cutting List

Location	Size to Cut
1	2¼" x 3"
2, 3	1¾" x 2½"
4, 5, 9, 10	1½" x 3¾"
8, 11	1½" x 2¾"
12, 13, 15, 16	1½" x 3
6, 7	1¼" x 2"
14	1" x 2½"

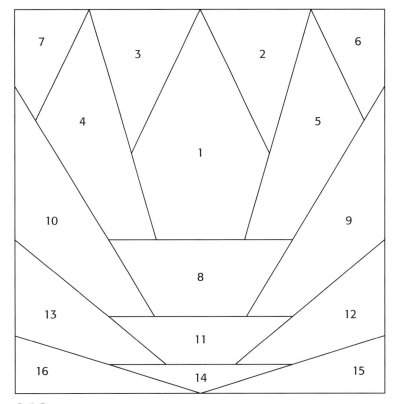

246

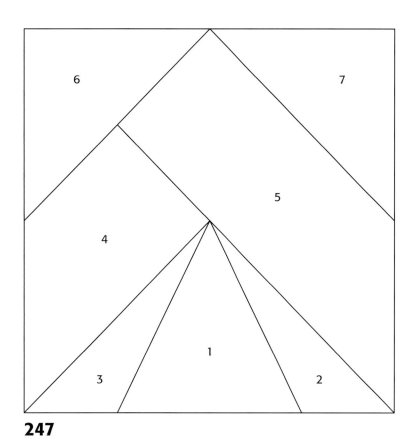

247

Block 247 Cutting List

Location	Size to Cut
6, 7	3¼" x 3¼" ◹
1	2¾" x 2¾"
5	2" x 4¾"
4	2" x 3½"
2, 3	1½" x 3½"

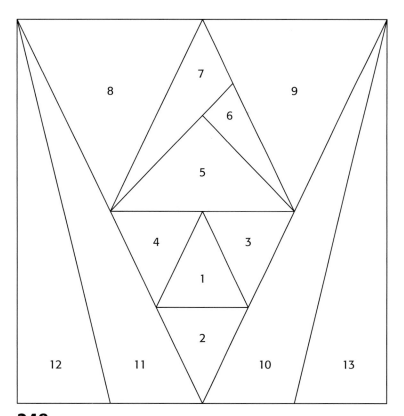

248

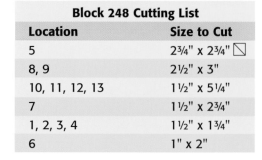

Block 248 Cutting List

Location	Size to Cut
5	2¾" x 2¾" ◹
8, 9	2½" x 3"
10, 11, 12, 13	1½" x 5¼"
7	1½" x 2¾"
1, 2, 3, 4	1½" x 1¾"
6	1" x 2"

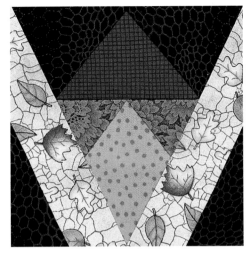

Block 249 Cutting List

Location	Size to Cut
1, 4	2¼" x 3¼"
5, 6	2¼" x 2¾"
7, 8	1½" x 5¼"
9, 10	1½" x 3"
2, 3	1½" x 2"

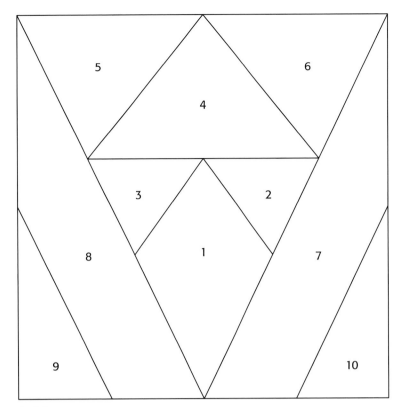

249

Block 250 Cutting List

Location	Size to Cut
1	2½" x 4½"
10	2" x 2" ⬦
3	1¼" x 5½"
4, 5	1¼" x 4¾"
2	1¼" x 4½"
6, 7	1¼" x 4"
8, 9	1¼" x 2½"

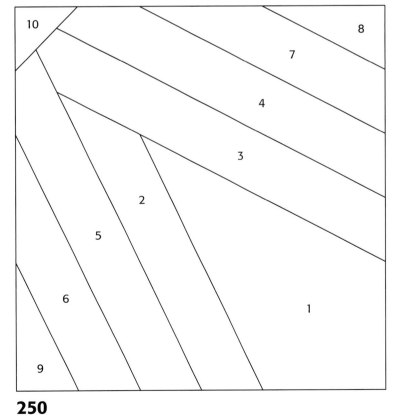

250

251

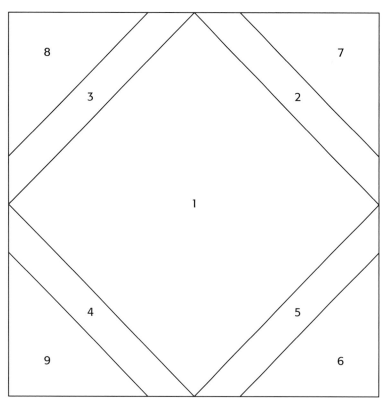

Block 251 Cutting List	
Location	**Size to Cut**
1	3½" x 3½"
6, 7, 8, 9	2¾" x 2¾" ◺
2, 3, 4, 5	1" x 4"

252

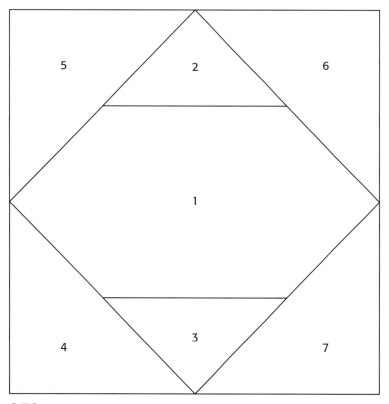

Block 252 Cutting List	
Location	**Size to Cut**
2, 3	3½" x 3½" ⊠
4, 5, 6, 7	3¼" x 3¼" ◺
1	2¾" x 4¾"

Block 253 Cutting List

Location	Size to Cut
2, 3	3½" x 3½" ⊠
1	2¾" x 4¾"
8, 9, 10, 11	2¼" x 2¼" ◺
4, 5, 6, 7	1½" x 4"

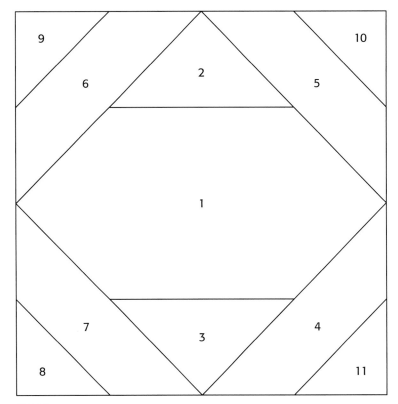

253

Block 254 Cutting List

Location	Size to Cut
8, 9, 10, 11	3¼" x 3¼" ◺
4, 5, 6, 7	2¾" x 2¾" ⊠
1	2" x 3¼"
2, 3	1¼" x 3½"

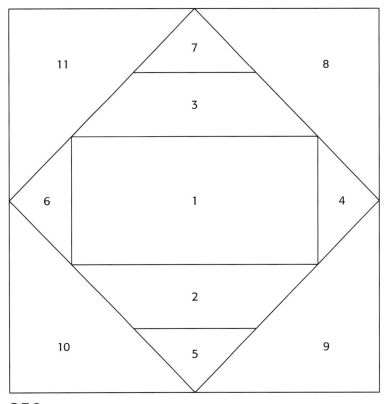

254

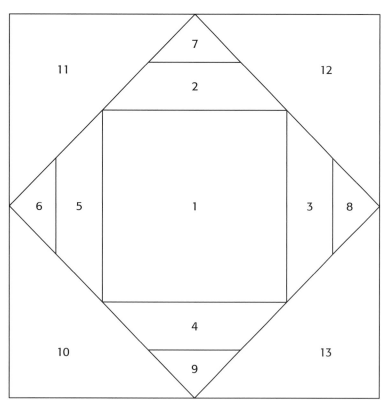

255

Block 255 Cutting List	
Location	**Size to Cut**
10, 11, 12, 13	3¼" x 3¼" ◲
1	2¾" x 2¾"
6, 7, 8, 9	2½" x 2½" ⊠
2, 3, 4, 5	1¼" x 3"

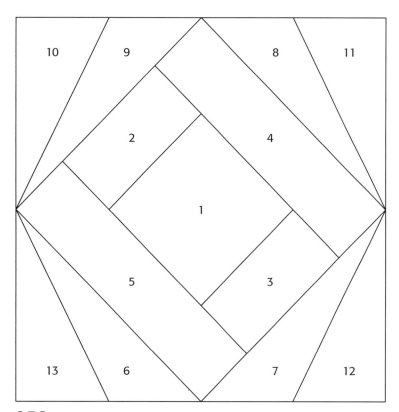

256

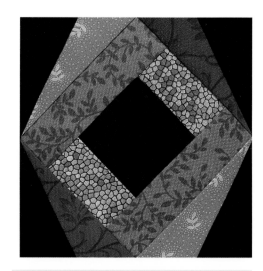

Block 256 Cutting List	
Location	**Size to Cut**
1	2" x 2"
10, 11, 12, 13	1½" x 3½"
6, 7, 8, 9	1¼" x 4"
4, 5	1¼" x 3½"
2, 3	1¼" x 2"

Block 257 Cutting List

Location	Size to Cut
1	3½" x 3½"
6, 7, 8, 9	1½" x 3½"
2, 3, 4, 5	1¼" x 4"

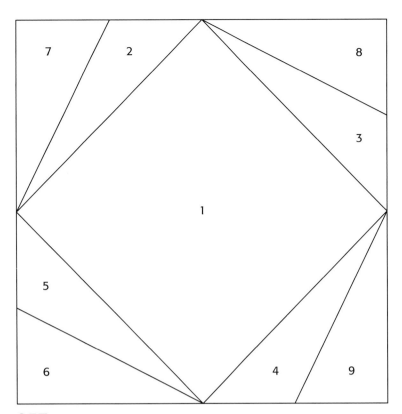

257

Block 258 Cutting List

Location	Size to Cut
2, 3, 4, 5	3" x 3" ⊠
10, 11, 12, 13	2½" x 2½" ◺
1	2" x 2"
9	1½" x 5"
7, 8	1½" x 3½"
6	1½" x 2½"

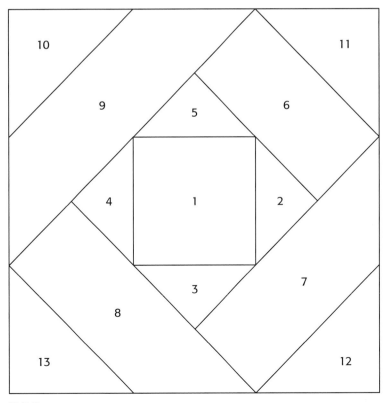

258

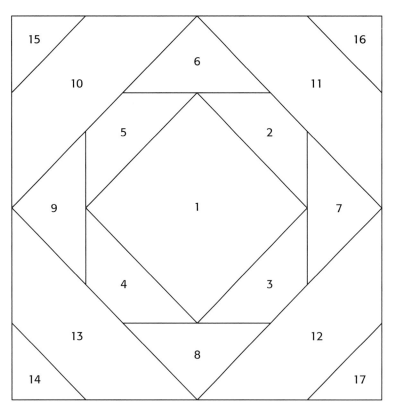

259

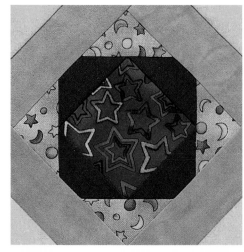

Block 259 Cutting List	
Location	**Size to Cut**
6, 7, 8, 9	3" x 3" ⊠
1	2¼" x 2¼"
14, 15, 16, 17	2" x 2" ◺
10, 11, 12, 13	1½" x 4"
2, 3, 4, 5	1¼" x 2½"

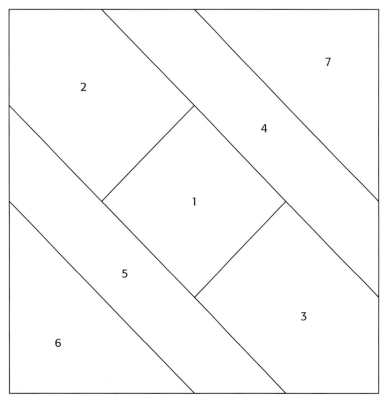

260

Block 260 Cutting List	
Location	**Size to Cut**
6, 7	3¼" x 3¼" ◺
2, 3	2" x 2¾"
1	2" x 2"
4, 5	1¼" x 5¼"

Block 261 Cutting List

Location	Size to Cut
10, 11, 12, 13, 18, 19, 20, 21	2½" x 2½" ◺
1	2" x 2"
14, 15, 16, 17	1¼" x 3¼"
6, 7, 8, 9	1¼" x 2¼"
2, 3, 4, 5	1¼" x 2"

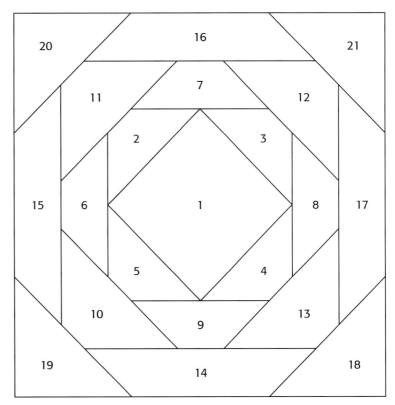

261

Block 262 Cutting List

Location	Size to Cut
6, 7	3½" x 3½" ⊠
2, 3, 4, 5, 8, 9, 10, 11, 14, 15, 16, 17	2¼" x 2¼" ◺
1	2" x 2"
12, 13	1¾" x 4¾"

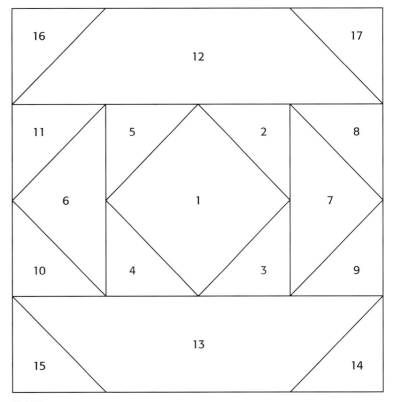

262

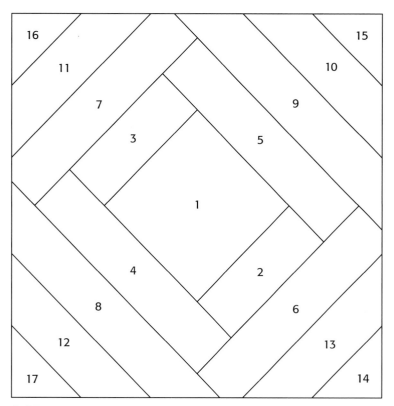

263

Block 263 Cutting List

Location	Size to Cut
1	2" x 2"
14, 15, 16, 17	2" x 2" ◹
8, 9	1¼" x 4¼"
4, 5, 6, 7, 10, 11, 12, 13	1¼" x 3¼"
2, 3	1¼" x 2"

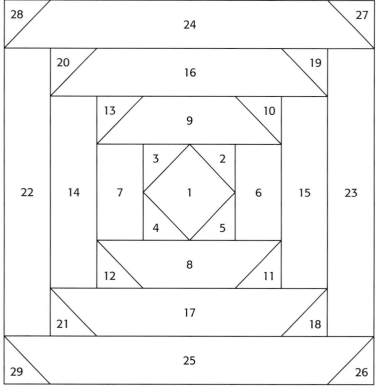

264

Block 264 Cutting List

Location	Size to Cut
2, 3, 4, 5, 10, 11, 12, 13, 18, 19, 20, 21, 26, 27, 28, 29	1¾" x 1¾" ◹
1	1½" x 1½"
24, 25	1¼" x 4¾"
16, 17, 22, 23	1¼" x 3¾"
8, 9, 14, 15	1¼" x 2¾"
6, 7	1¼" x 1¾"

Block 265 Cutting List

Location	Size to Cut
2, 3, 8, 9	2¾" x 2¾" ◨
4, 5	2" x 3¼"
1	2" x 2"
6, 7	1½" x 5"

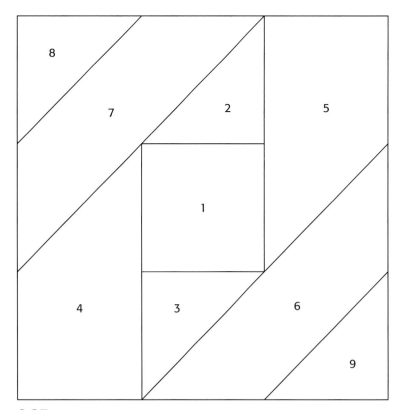

265

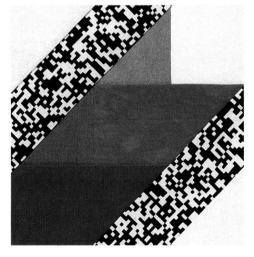

Block 266 Cutting List

Location	Size to Cut
2, 4, 8, 9	2¾" x 2¾" ◨
3, 5	2" x 3¼"
1	2" x 2"
6, 7	1½" x 5"

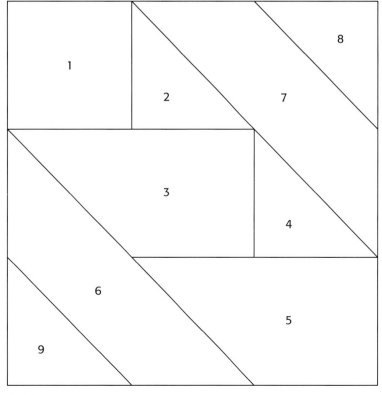

266

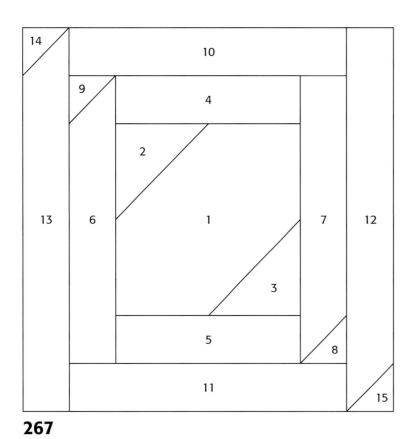

267

Block 267 Cutting List

Location	Size to Cut
2, 3	2¼" x 2¼" ◺
1	2" x 3½"
8, 9, 14, 15	1¾" x 1¾" ◺
12, 13	1¼" x 4¾"
6, 7, 10, 11	1¼" x 3¾"
4, 5	1¼" x 2¾"

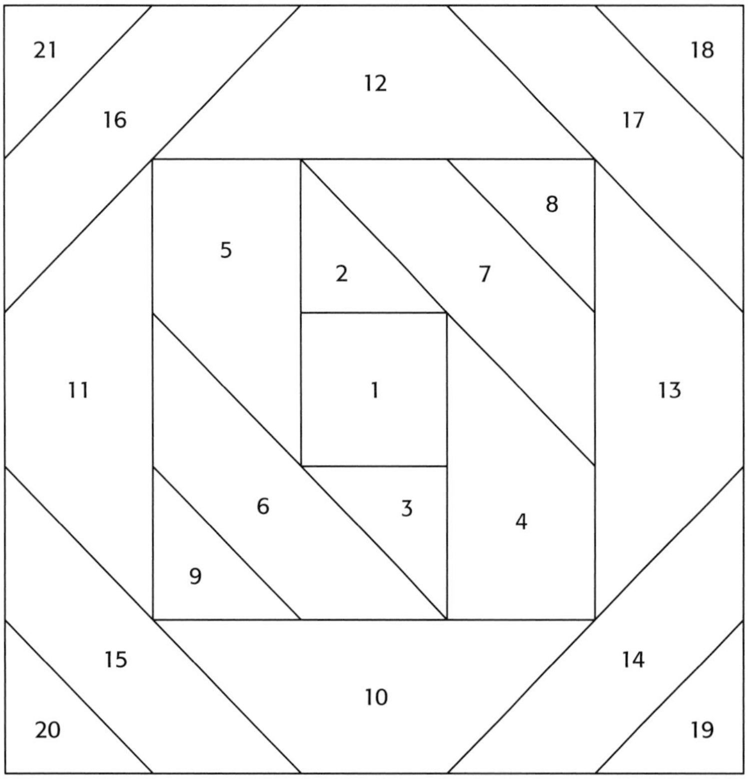

268

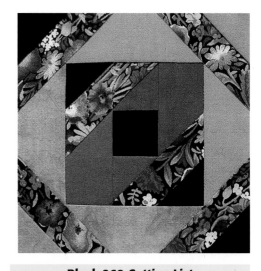

Block 268 Cutting List

Location	Size to Cut
2, 3, 8, 9, 18, 19, 20, 21	2" x 2" ◺
10, 11, 12, 13	1½" x 3"
4, 5	1½" x 2¼"
1	1½" x 1½"
14, 15, 16, 17	1¼" x 3¼"
6, 7	1¼" x 3"

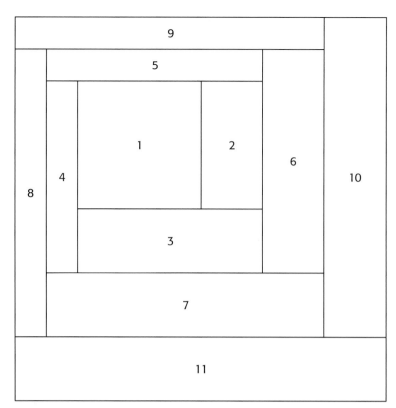

269

Block 269 Cutting List

Location	Size to Cut
1	2" x 2"
11	1¼" x 4¾"
10	1¼" x 4"
7	1¼" x 3¾"
3, 6	1¼" x 3"
2	1¼" x 2"
8, 9	1" x 4"
4, 5	1" x 3"

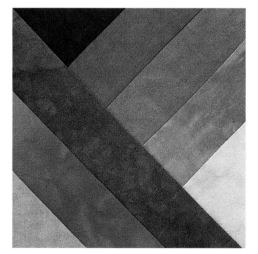

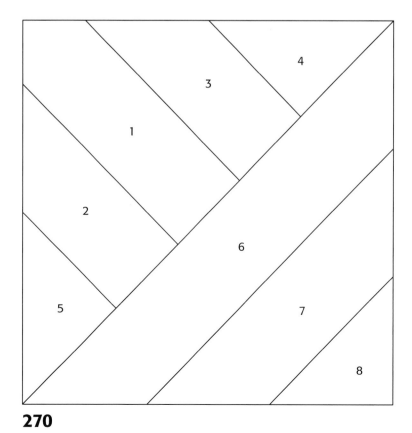

270

Block 270 Cutting List

Location	Size to Cut
4, 5	2¾" x 2¾" ◺
8	2½" x 2½" ◺
6	1½" x 6½"
7	1½" x 5"
1	1½" x 3½"
2, 3	1½" x 3"

271

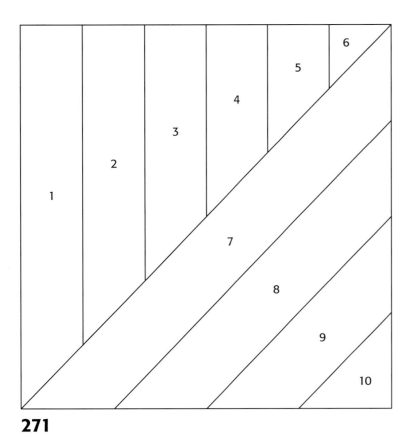

Block 271 Cutting List

Location	Size to Cut
6, 10	2¼" x 2¼" ◹
7	1¼" x 6½"
8	1¼" x 5½"
1	1¼" x 4¾"
2, 9	1¼" x 4"
3	1¼" x 3½"
4	1¼" x 2¾"
5	1¼" x 2"

272

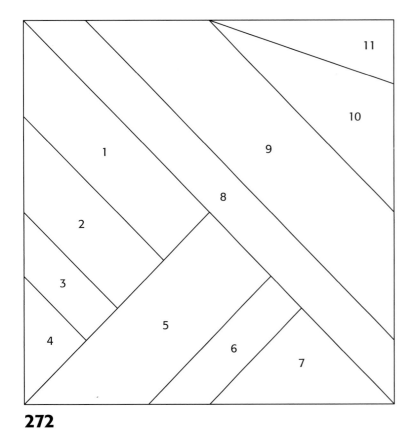

Block 272 Cutting List

Location	Size to Cut
7	2¾" x 2¾" ◹
4	2¼" x 2¼" ◹
9	1½" x 6"
5, 10	1½" x 4"
8	1¼" x 6½"
1, 11	1¼" x 3½"
2, 6	1¼" x 2¾"
3	1¼" x 2¼"

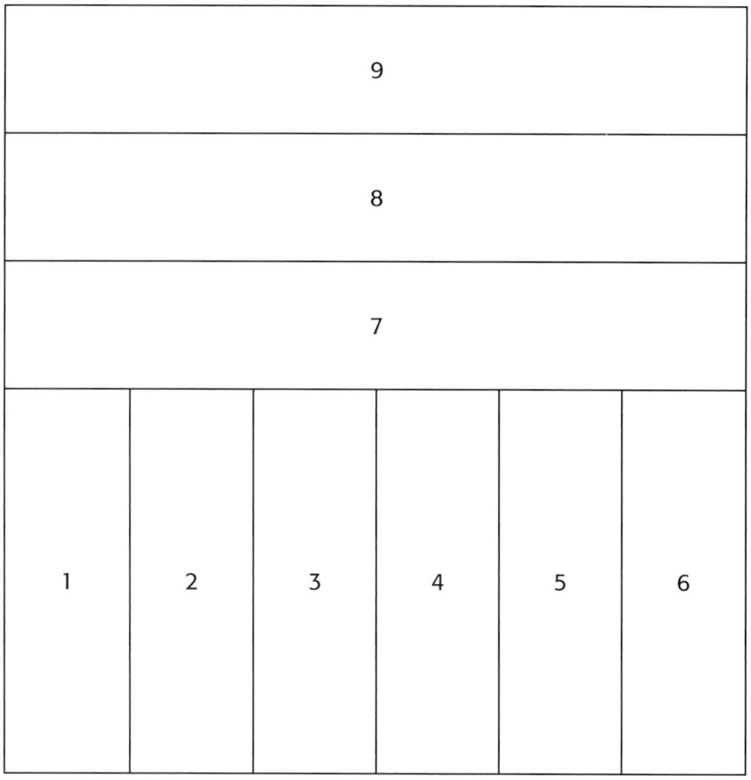

Block 273 Cutting List

Location	Size to Cut
7, 8, 9	1¼" x 4¾"
1, 2, 3, 4, 5, 6	1¼" x 2¾"

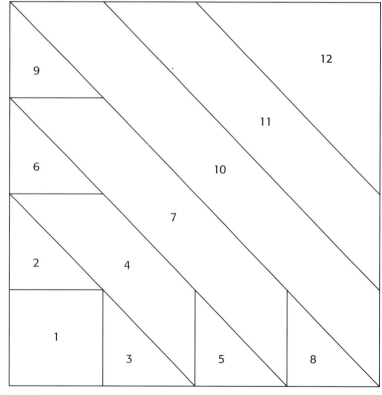

273

Block 274 Cutting List

Location	Size to Cut
12	3¼" x 3¼" ◱
2, 3, 5, 6, 8, 9	2¼" x 2¼" ◱
1	1¾" x 1¾"
10	1¼" x 6½"
11	1¼" x 5½"
7	1¼" x 5"
4	1¼" x 3½"

274

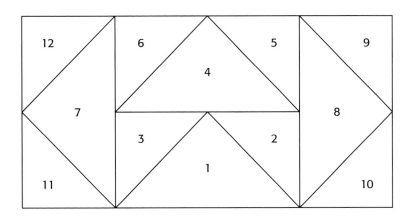

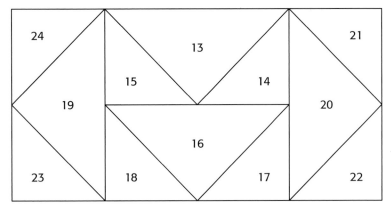

Block 275 Cutting List

Location	Size to Cut
1, 4, 7, 8, 13, 16, 19, 20	3½" x 3½" ⊠
2, 3, 5, 6, 9, 10, 11, 12, 14, 15, 17, 18, 21, 22, 23, 24	2¼" x 2¼" ◺

275

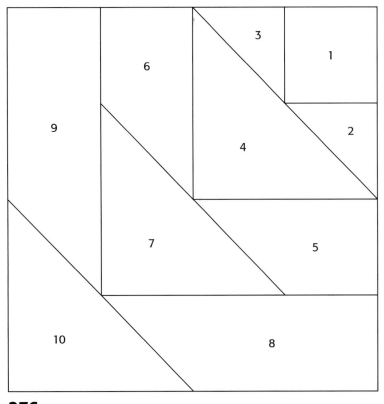

Block 276 Cutting List

Location	Size to Cut
4, 7, 10	3¼" x 3¼" ◺
2, 3	2¼" x 2¼" ◺
8, 9	1¾" x 3¾"
5, 6	1¾" x 2¾"
1	1¾" x 1¾"

276

Block 277 Cutting List

Location	Size to Cut
1, 4	2¾" x 2¾"
2, 3, 5, 6	2¼" x 2¼" ◺
7	2" x 6½"

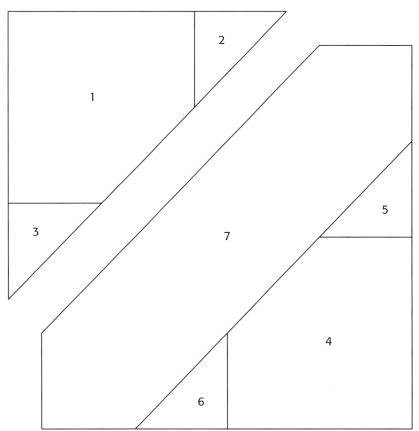

277

Block 278 Cutting List

Location	Size to Cut
1, 4, 7, 10	3½" x 3½" ⊠
2, 3, 5, 6, 8, 9, 11, 12	2¼" x 2¼" ◺
13, 14	1¾" x 4¾"

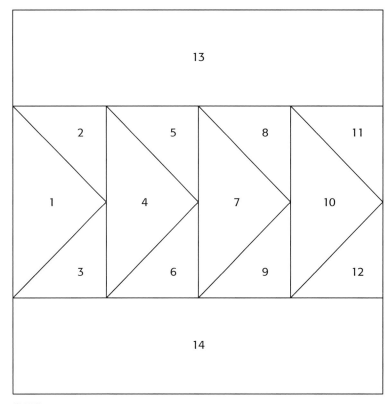

278

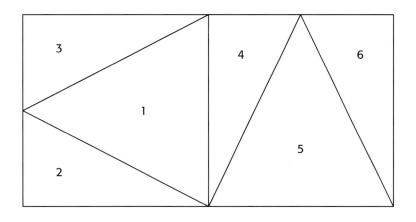

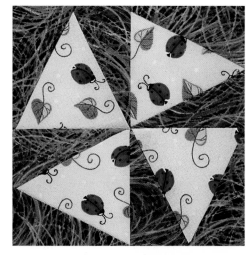

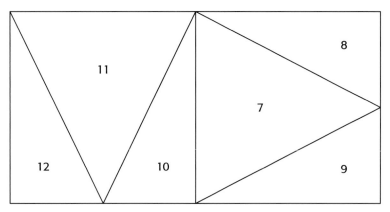

279

Block 279 Cutting List	
Location	**Size to Cut**
1, 7	2¾" x 2¾"
5, 11	2½" x 3¼"
4, 10	1¾" x 2¾"
2, 3, 6, 8, 9, 12	1½" x 3"

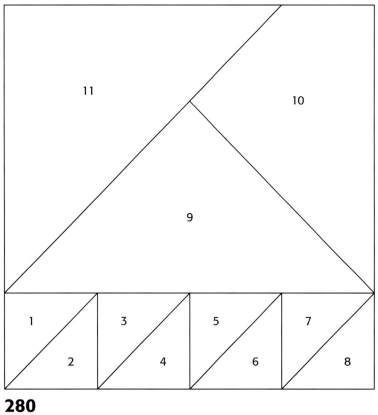

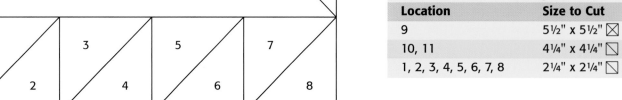

280

Block 280 Cutting List	
Location	**Size to Cut**
9	5½" x 5½" ⊠
10, 11	4¼" x 4¼" ⧅
1, 2, 3, 4, 5, 6, 7, 8	2¼" x 2¼" ⧅

Block 281 Cutting List

Location	Size to Cut
1, 2, 3, 4, 5, 6, 7, 8	3¼" x 3¼" ◲

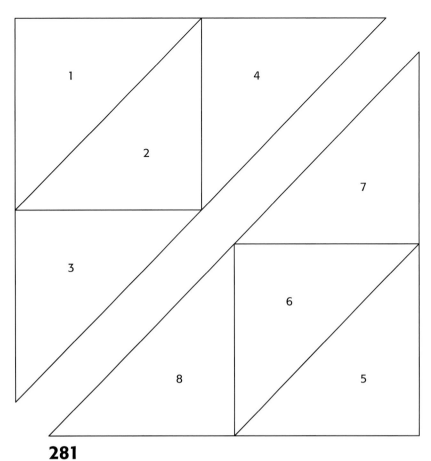

281

Block 282 Cutting List

Location	Size to Cut
3, 4, 5, 6	2½" x 2½" ⊠
1, 2, 7, 8, 9, 10, 15, 16, 17, 18, 23, 24, 25, 26	2¼" x 2¼" ◲
19, 20, 21, 22	1¼" x 3¾"
11, 12, 13, 14	1¼" x 2¾"

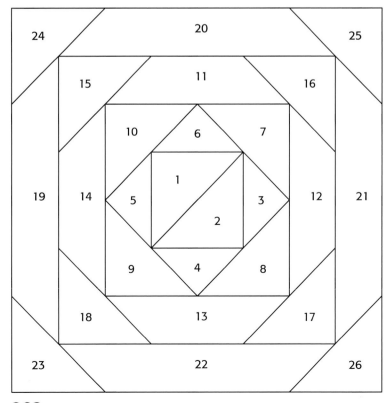

282

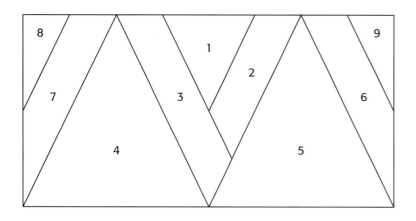

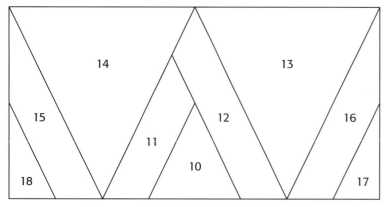

Block 283 Cutting List

Location	Size to Cut
4, 5, 13, 14	2½" x 3"
1, 10	1¾" x 1¾"
3, 6, 7, 12, 15, 16	1" x 3"
2, 8, 9, 11, 17, 18	1" x 2½"

283

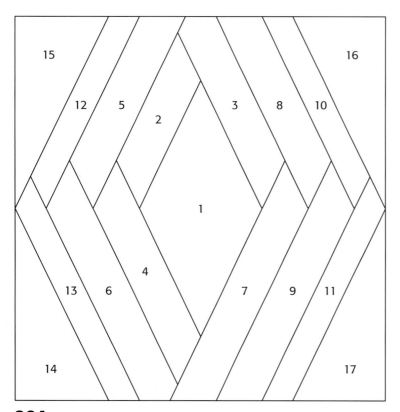

Block 284 Cutting List

Location	Size to Cut
1	2" x 3¼"
14, 15, 16, 17	1½" x 3½"
6, 7, 9, 11, 13	1" x 3½"
3, 4, 5, 8, 10, 12	1" x 3"
2	1" x 2½"

284

Block 285 Cutting List

Location	Size to Cut
1, 2, 4, 5, 7, 8, 10, 11	3½" x 3½" ⊠
3, 6, 9, 12	3¼" x 3¼" ◺

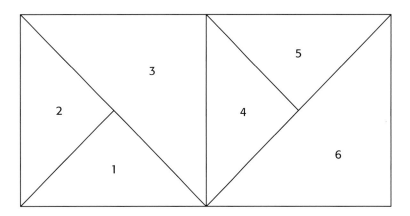

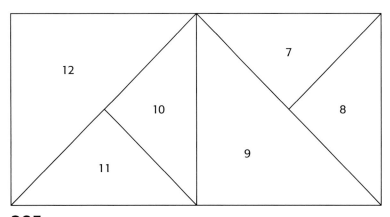

285

Block 286 Cutting List

Location	Size to Cut
4	5¼" x 5¼" ⊠
2, 3, 5, 6	3¼" x 3¼" ◺
1	2" x 5"

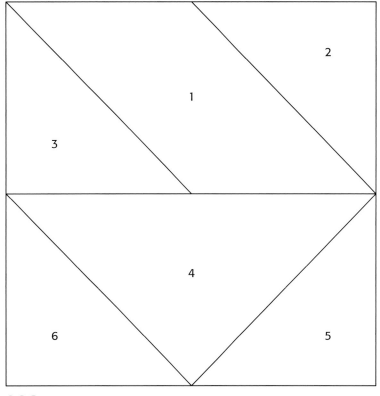

286

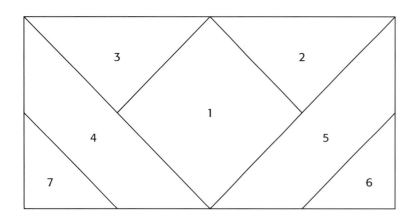

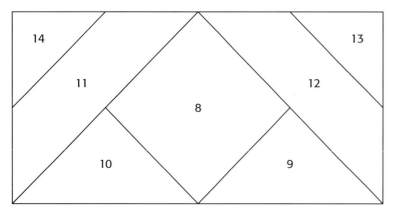

287

Block 287 Cutting List

Location	Size to Cut	
2, 3, 9, 10	3½" x 3½"	⊠
6, 7, 13, 14	2¼" x 2¼"	◺
1, 8	2" x 2"	
4, 5, 11, 12	1¼" x 3½"	

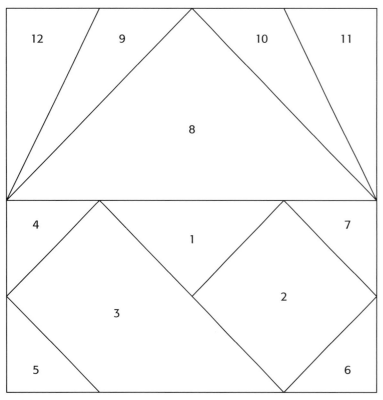

288

Block 288 Cutting List

Location	Size to Cut	
8	5½" x 5½"	⊠
1	3½" x 3½"	⊠
4, 5, 6, 7	2¼" x 2¼"	◺
3	2" x 3¾"	
2	2" x 2"	
9, 10	1½" x 3¾"	
11, 12	1½" x 3½"	

Block 289 Cutting List

Location	Size to Cut
1, 4, 5, 6, 7, 8	3¼" x 3¼" ◹
2, 3	1¾" x 3¾"

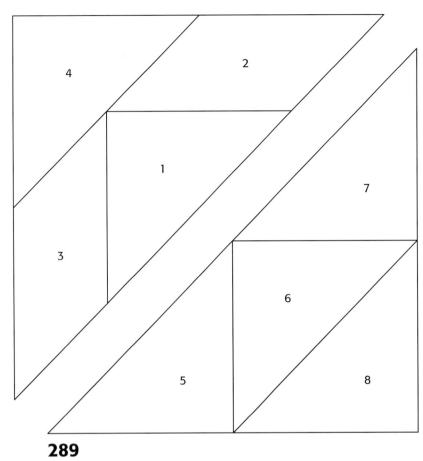

289

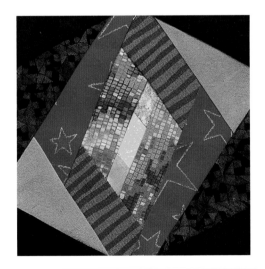

Block 290 Cutting List

Location	Size to Cut
8, 9	1½" x 4"
12, 13	1½" x 3¾"
10, 11	1½" x 3½"
14, 15, 16, 17	1½" x 3"
4, 5, 6, 7	1¼" x 3"
1, 2, 3	1" x 1½"

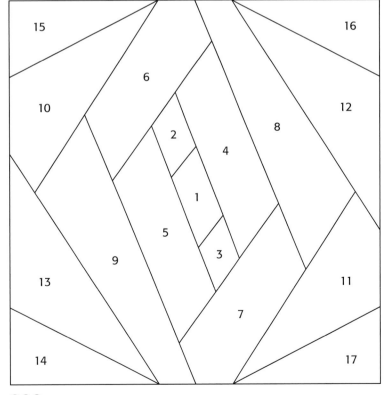

290

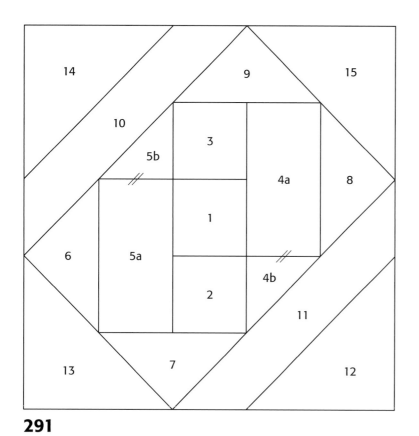

291

Block 291 Cutting List	
Location	**Size to Cut**
6, 7, 8, 9	3¼" x 3¼" ⊠
12, 13, 14, 15	3" x 3" ◹
4b, 5b	2" x 2" ◹
4a, 5a	1½" x 2¼"
1, 2, 3	1½" x 1½"
10, 11	1¼" x 5"

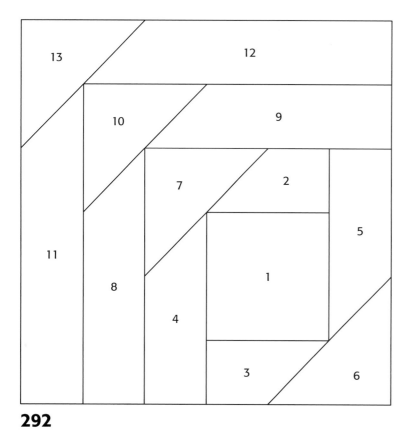

292

Block 292 Cutting List	
Location	**Size to Cut**
6, 7, 10, 13	2¾" x 2¾" ◹
1	2" x 2"
11, 12	1¼" x 4"
8, 9	1¼" x 3½"
4, 5	1¼" x 2½"
2, 3	1¼" x 2"

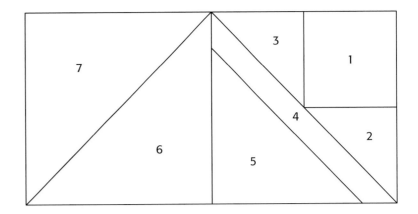

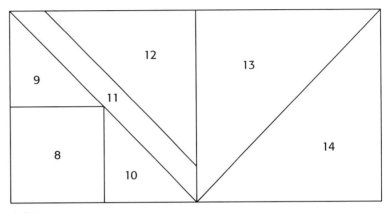

293

Block 293 Cutting List

Location	Size to Cut
6, 7, 13, 14	3¼" x 3¼" ◹
5, 12	3" x 3" ◹
2, 3, 9, 10	2¼" x 2¼" ◹
1, 8	1¾" x 1¾"
4, 11	1" x 3½"

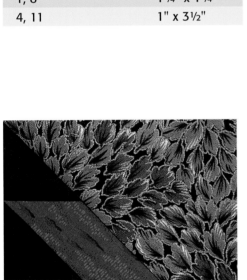

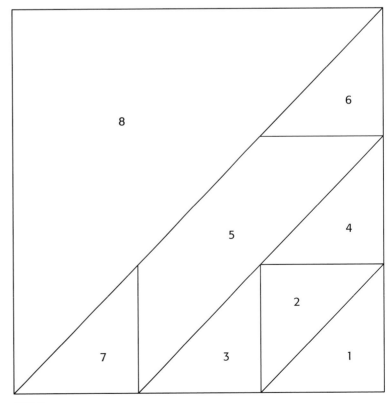

294

Block 294 Cutting List

Location	Size to Cut
8	5¼" x 5¼" ◹
1, 2, 3, 4, 6, 7	2¾" x 2¾" ◹
5	1½" x 5"

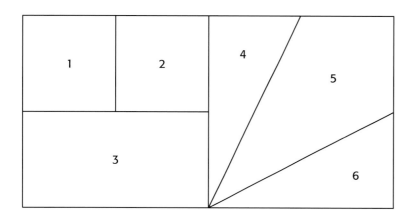

295

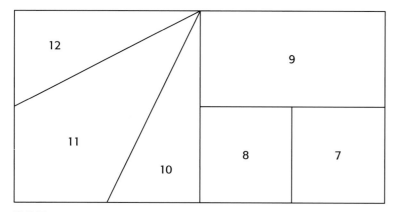

Block 295 Cutting List

Location	Size to Cut
5, 11	2" x 3½"
3, 4, 9, 10	1¾" x 2¾"
1, 2, 7, 8	1¾" x 1¾"
6, 12	1½" x 3½"

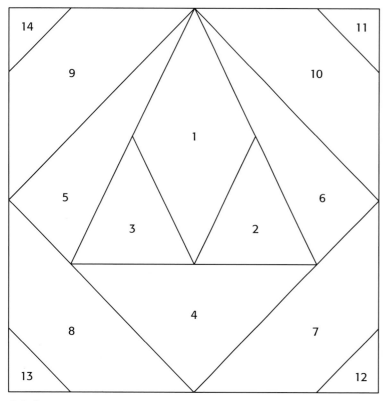

296

Block 296 Cutting List

Location	Size to Cut
4	4¼" x 4¼" ⊠
7, 8, 9, 10	3¼" x 3¼" ◻
1	2" x 3¼"
11, 12, 13, 14	2" x 2" ◻
2, 3	1¾" x 2¼"
5, 6	1½" x 3¾"

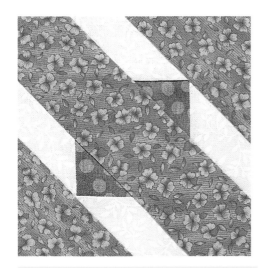

Block 297 Cutting List

Location	Size to Cut
4, 8	3¼" x 3¼" ◺
1, 5	2¼" x 2¼" ◺
9	2" x 6½"
2, 3, 6, 7	1¾" x 2½"

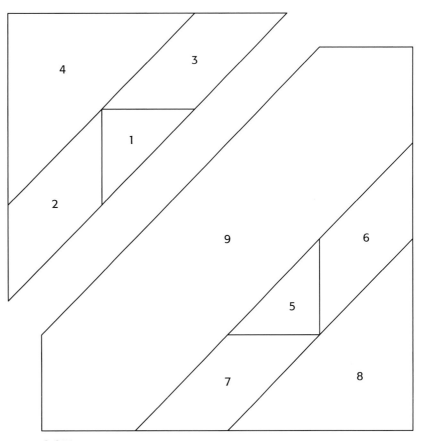

297

Block 298 Cutting List

Location	Size to Cut
10	2¼" x 2¼" ◺
8, 9	2" x 4½"
1	2" x 3½"
7	1¾" x 3½"
6	1¾" x 2¾"
2, 3, 4, 5	1¼" x 3¾"

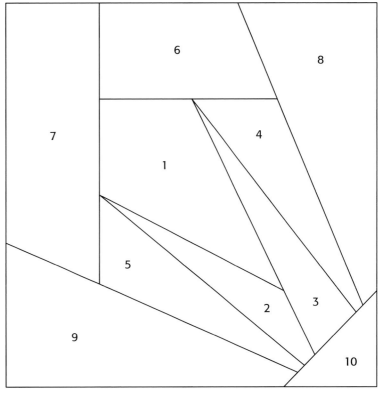

298

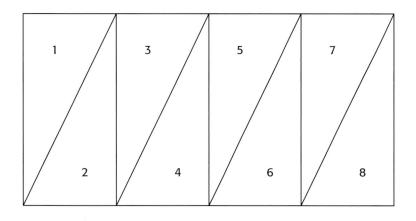

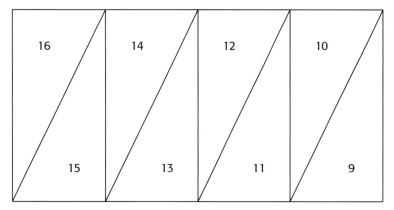

299

Block 299 Cutting List	
Location	**Size to Cut**
1, 3, 5, 7, 9, 11, 13, 15	1¾" x 2¾"
2, 4, 6, 8, 10, 12, 14, 16	1½" x 3"

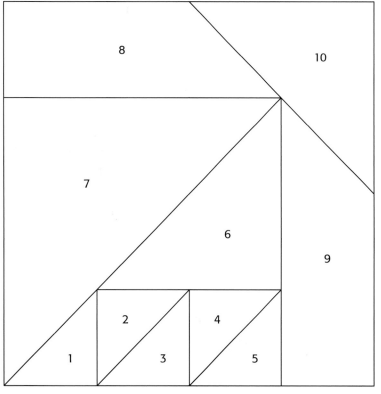

300

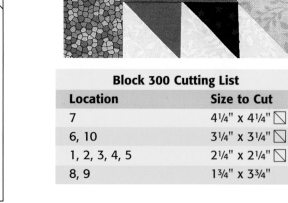

Block 300 Cutting List	
Location	**Size to Cut**
7	4¼" x 4¼" ◺
6, 10	3¼" x 3¼" ◺
1, 2, 3, 4, 5	2¼" x 2¼" ◺
8, 9	1¾" x 3¾"

RESOURCES

**Add-A-Quarter Ruler and
Add-An-Eighth Ruler**
C M Designs
7968 Kelty Trail
Franktown, CO 80116
Phone: 303-841-5920

Thread-Clipping Snips
Tool-Tron Industries
Phone: 830-249-8277
Web site: www.Tooltron.com
Email: tooltron@texas.net

Carol Doak Web Site
Carol Doak's newsletter and teaching schedule are available on her Web site at the following address: http://quilt.com/CDoak

ABOUT THE AUTHOR

As a bestselling author, celebrated teacher, and award-winning quiltmaker, Carol Doak has greatly influenced the art and craft of quiltmaking for more than a decade, both in the United States and internationally. Her accomplishments include a sizable collection of popular books: *Easy Machine Paper Piecing, Easy Paper-Pieced Baby Quilts, Show Me How to Paper Piece, Easy Paper-Pieced Miniatures, Your First Quilt Book (or it should be!), Easy Stash Quilts, 50 Fabulous Paper-Pieced Stars,* and *40 Bright & Bold Paper-Pieced Blocks.* It is no secret that Carol has helped raise the popularity of paper piecing, her trademark technique, through her innovative designs and easy-to-follow instructions.

An impressive range of Carol's beautiful blue-ribbon quilts has been featured in several books and magazines.

As a teacher, Carol is known for her infectious enthusiasm for quiltmaking. She has a gift for sharing her inspiring ideas and techniques with her students in a positive and unique way.

Carol lives with her husband in Windham, New Hampshire, and is often traveling the world sharing her love of quilting with others.

6/04